MAGDALEN COLLEGE
AND THE CROWN

D1471714

PRESIDENT HOUGH BEFORE THE COMMISSIONERS
centre and right: Hough and the Fellows; left: the Commissioners,
Bishop Cartwright, flanked by Wright and Jenner

Magdalen College and the Crown

Essays for the Tercentenary of
the Restoration of the College
1688

✳

LAURENCE BROCKLISS

GERALD HARRISS

AND

ANGUS MACINTYRE

✳

Printed for the College

OXFORD 1988

ISBN 0 9513747 0 2

Printed in Great Britain

CONTENTS

PLATES

PREFACE

On 25th October 1688, after a long and hard-fought contest with James II and his government, there took place the 'Restoration' of the President, Fellows and Demies of the College. The tercentenary of this remarkable episode in the College's history, when Magdalen's fortunes were of national importance, has provided the occasion for the publication of these essays. As Fellows in Modern History we were glad to accept the invitation to write them. We have written them independently and allowed any nuances of difference in our interpretations to stand. Such differences are inseparable from the study of the past. We hope that our essays will be of interest to past and present members of the College, to all those benefactors whose generosity has enabled the College in recent years to restore the Tower and our other ancient buildings, and to those members of the general public who love and visit the College.

On the College's behalf, we record our gratitude to the Magdalen College Development Trust for its generous support towards the costs of publication. Quotations from the College's archival materials are made with the permission of the President and Fellows. For permission to reproduce the bas-relief on President Hough's monument, we thank the Dean and Chapter of Worcester Cathedral. We thank Thomas-Photos, Oxford (plate 1) and Mr M. R. Dudley (frontispiece, plates 2, 3 and 4) for their photographs. We are grateful to John Stoye, Hugo Brunner, and Dr Janie Cottis, Archivist of the College, for their advice and assistance.

L.W.B.B.
G.L.H.
A.D.M.

A LOYAL BUT TROUBLESOME COLLEGE 1458-1672

*

GERALD HARRISS

Magdalen College owed its foundation indirectly to royal patronage. When Henry VI promoted William Waynflete from the relatively humble post of headmaster of Winchester College to be the first provost of his new foundation at Eton, and a few years later bishop of Winchester, he afforded him the opportunity to found the best endowed of the medieval Oxford colleges. Before Henry's reign ended in 1461 Waynflete had held the office of chancellor and used his influence at the royal and papal courts to transfer the properties and site of the hospital of St John the Baptist to his new foundation. Although the political vicissitudes of the Wars of the Roses endangered the existence of the college for over a decade, by 1469 Waynflete had gained the support of Edward IV for the survival of Eton and was ready to proceed with the building of Magdalen.[1] Waynflete himself had chosen the first president of his college, William Tybard, in 1458, and when the buildings were complete and the college had been brought under the jurisdiction of the bishop of Winchester as its Visitor, he replaced Tybard with a new president, Richard Mayew, in 1480. Before he died in 1486 Waynflete established the college as a self-governing institution, giving it a landed endowment, a library, and a set of statutes.

For the next twenty years, the college flourished under

1. The standard life of Waynflete is R. Chandler, *The Life of William Waynflete* (London, 1811). For a brief summary of his foundation of the college, see Gerald Harriss, 'William Waynflete and the foundation of the college', *Magdalen College Record* (1986), 33-37. An extensive examination of the early years of the college has been made by J. Mills, 'The foundation, endowment, and early administration of Magdalen College, Oxford', unpublished B. Litt. thesis (Oxford, 1973).

Mayew's rule and became the centre for the new classical learning at Oxford. Grocyn lectured there between 1483 and 1488 and its school pioneered new methods of teaching Latin Grammar. Favoured by Henry VII, who granted it exemption from taxation, the college purchased further estates and its income touched £900 p.a. The tower rose, a monument to its president's own ascending career. Waynflete's last years had been honoured by visits to the college of Edward IV and Richard III; in 1488 Mayew welcomed Henry VII and in 1495 the heir apparent, Prince Arthur, while he himself frequented the court where the Visitor, Bishop Foxe, was Lord Privy Seal. In 1490 he was sent to Spain to open negotiations for the marriage of Prince Henry and Catherine of Aragon, and on his return became the king's chaplain and, by 1497, royal almoner. Although he was now less frequently in college, his influence served it well, as the fine tapestries which he received as a gift for his services remind us to this day. By 1504 he had become bishop of Hereford, a coveted dignity, but one which the revenues of the see were scarcely able to support. Now aged about 65, he preferred to reside in Magdalen and sustain his episcopal state from its resources. Soon there were mutterings amongst the fellows, complaining of his neglect and of disorder in the college's affairs. Money had disappeared from the college chest in 1503 and the affair was never cleared up. On 20 January 1507, on appeal from some of the fellows, Foxe intervened and deprived Mayew of the presidency.[2]

With the office vacant, the fellows were bound by the statutes to commence the process of election within two days and to complete it before the lapse of a further fifteen. Only those who were or had been fellows of Magdalen or New College were eligible. All the fellows were to vote at the first scrutiny, each proposing two names; then from those nominated the thirteen senior fellows were to make the final choice, usually of the candidate with the largest number of votes. They were to be guided by the Holy Spirit, without concern for worldly fear or favour. No details survive of this first election, but it was evidently properly carried out and John

2. H. A. Wilson, *Magdalen College* (London, 1899), 45-59; A. B. Emden, *A Biographical Register of the University of Oxford to 1500* (Oxford, 1958), ii. 1247-9 (hereafter cited as *BRUO*).

Veysey was elected. At the time he was archdeacon of both Chester and Barnstaple, a considerable pluralist who was subsequently to stand in great favour with Henry VIII as a court chaplain, becoming dean of Windsor and finally bishop of Exeter. Perhaps he was already too much the courtier for Foxe's liking, for as Visitor he declined to confirm the choice and on 20 April sent a letter announcing Veysey's resignation and instructing the fellows to proceed to a new election. John Claymond, whom they now elected, was a humanist and the friend of Erasmus; clearly he was Foxe's nominee, for nine years later he moved to Corpus Christi as the first president of Foxe's new college.[3]

By then Foxe and the other old councillors of Henry VII had been displaced by the rising star of Thomas Wolsey, a former fellow and bursar of Magdalen. Not surprisingly it was his voice which determined the next two elections. The first, on 7 December 1516, was that of John Higdon, one of the bursars in 1503 who was well known to Wolsey. There are no details of the voting, but the fellows subsequently wrote to Wolsey thanking him for recommending Higdon.[4] The same story was repeated nine years later when Wolsey transferred Higdon to his new foundation, Cardinal College (later Christ Church), as dean, at the same time recommending a successor at Magdalen. This was Lawrence Stubbs, a long-standing member of the cardinal's household, who had also followed Wolsey in the office of bursar. Although the fellows reminded the cardinal that their oath to be led solely by the motion of the Holy Spirit forbade them to make any promises, they did, on 22 November, duly elect Stubbs as president. Stubbs seems to have continued in Wolsey's household until 1527, and it was perhaps dissatisfaction with this that lay behind what looks like an attempt to unseat him by an appeal to the aged Foxe as Visitor. Early in February 1527 the vice-president wrote to Foxe announcing that Stubbs had resigned on 16 January and

---

3. W. D. Macray, *A Register of the Members of St Mary Magdalen College, Oxford* 8 vols. (Oxford, 1894-1915), iv. 110-12, 179; *BRUO*, iii. 1947-8 (Veysey); i. 428-30 (Claymond).

4. J. R. Bloxam, *A Register of the Presidents, Fellows, Demies etc. of St Mary Magdalen College* 7 vols. (Oxford, 1853-85), iv. p. xxiv; Macray, *Register*, i. 70; *BRUO* ii. 931.

describing how, in due form, John Burgess had been elected in his place. Burgess indeed issued one document as president, on 10 July, duly entered in the college register; but other documents under Stubbs's name as president were dated in February and again in August 1527.[5] For Wolsey was not prepared to see his client displaced in this way, and he insisted on restoring Stubbs to the presidency, overriding Foxe by his legatine authority. The record of those voting for Burgess was hastily erased from the college register. However Stubbs enjoyed only a brief restitution, for by April 1528 a new president, Thomas Knolles, was in office, though the register contains no record of his election. Knolles was a Yorkshireman, vicar of Wakefield and sub-dean of York; he had not been a fellow for 25 years and could hardly have been known in the college. Like his predecessors he had held the office of bursar, in 1501-2, and probably owed his nomination to Wolsey, as archbishop of York. One thing is certain: he was a staunch traditionalist in religious matters at a time when radical opinions were infiltrating Wolsey's own foundation and when the issues of Henry VIII's divorce and supremacy over the church in England were already casting an ominous shadow.[6]

The choice of this undistinguished figure marks a hiatus between two periods in which the circumstances and character of election to the presidency radically changed. Rivalled only by Christ Church in wealth and prestige, Magdalen was bound to attract the attention of those with power and patronage in church and state. Hitherto the office of president had been filled by the recommendation of the greatest in the church. Some of those who had occupied it were learned and devout, and governed the college well, but for all except Knolles Magdalen was a stepping stone to higher preferment. It was a typical staging post for the ambitious, along with canonries, deanships,

5. The account given here differs from that in Bloxam, *Register*, iv. 45-6 and Macray, *Register*, i. 128-9, 141-2. *BRUO*, iii. 1809 gives a different sequence but the references given are not reliable. The election of Burgess is entered in Magdalen College Archives, Register B, fos. 60-60v, 155. Documents issued under the name of Stubbs are on fos. 30, 31,45, 46, 48, 68, 158; the document of 10 July 1527 in the name of Burgess is on fo. 157.

6. Macray, *Register*, i. 130-3; *BRUO*, ii. 1060. The last document in Register B issued by Stubbs was dated 6 April 1528 (fo. 45) and the first by Knolles was dated 17 April 1528 (fo. 69).

and other middle ranking offices within the church, in which residence was not required. Though they may have disapproved, the fellows had not (except perhaps in 1527) openly demurred at the absorption of the college presidency into the patronage network, for connections with the great undoubtedly brought benefits collectively and individually. But now Henry VIII's breach with papal authority introduced another dimension. Ineluctably the church of England became the embattled enemy of Rome, and its members were required to affirm their loyalty to the crown under statutory oath. The colleges in Oxford and Cambridge remained the fount of theological learning and nurseries for the priesthood, but henceforth they would need to be carefully monitored and to be ruled by men of reliable opinions. Thus the crown itself now began to take an interest in who was appointed, not merely as a means of reward and advancement for its servants but as a measure of religious and political control. Nor was it content to leave this to the church; in 1535 Thomas Cromwell issued the first commission for the reform of the universities. All this enhanced the importance and influence of heads of houses in the government of the university, but it also provoked opposition and division within colleges.[7] In the latter part of the century religious change and diversity fuelled splits between senior and junior fellows, and nowhere more than at Magdalen which had become the cradle of puritanism within the university.

The first sign of this new climate came in 1535. Alongside the visitation of the university, Cromwell made the first attempt to remove a sitting president and replace him with a crown nominee. No charges were brought against Thomas Knolles, and it is not apparent why he had become unacceptable, but he had been one of those who had delivered the university's opinion on the validity of the king's proposed divorce in 1531, and his reservations may have drawn him to Cromwell's attention. His will reveals him as devoted to the old observances, and he had recently spent a large sum on the adornment of the high altar of the chapel. Perhaps, too, he was

7. Claire Cross, 'Oxford and the Tudor state, 1509-1558', in *The History of the University of Oxford*: vol. iii: *The Collegiate University*, ed. J. K. McConica (Oxford, 1986), 126.

not unhappy to return to his native Wakefield where he intended to be buried alongside his parents. At any rate by 1535 Cromwell had procured his readiness to resign in favour of Thomas Marshall, one of those scholars whom, along with Thomas Starkey, Cromwell had recruited from Magdalen as propagandists for the royal supremacy. But the fellows indicated their unwillingness to elect Marshall, and by January 1536 Cromwell had found a new candidate, Owen Oglethorpe. Oglethorpe was a younger and more distinguished man than Marshall and praelector in moral philosophy. The fellows undertook to elect him on the death of Knolles, but within a month Knolles had resigned (3 February) and Oglethorpe was unanimously elected.[8] Oglethorpe was a catholic in the Henrician mode, acceptable to the old king to whom he owed his promotion to the deanery of Windsor in 1540 and whose effigy he placed on the splendid panelling installed behind the dais in the hall in the following year. But he was out of sympathy with the radical protestantism of Edward VI's reign, and under his presidency the college experienced to the full the disruptive effects of the religious changes which now commenced.

The first days of the new reign saw violent demonstrations against the Mass in the college chapel by the younger and more extreme fellows.[9] Oglethorpe found himself in a difficult position. The government, under Protector Somerset, was encouraging reformation in religion while reproving the college for its indiscipline. The junior fellows denounced Oglethorpe to the privy council for failing to proceed with the reforms, while the president and some of the senior fellows suspected the council of inciting the college to depart from its statutes in order to procure its dissolution. In this atmosphere of confusion and mistrust the appointment of a further commission to visit the university confirmed their fears. The commissioners were equally concerned to eradicate popish ceremonies and to uphold order and authority against undisciplined attempts at reform. They issued 44 injunctions for the reform of life and worship within the college. Already in Magdalen chapel

8. Macray, *Register*, i. 130-3, 169-70, ii. 55; Magdalen College Archives, Register C, fos. 71-2.

9. Wilson, *Magdalen College*, 87-88.

ornaments had been removed and the services changed, and the commission now ordered the conversion of benefactions for masses into exhibitions for scholars. It also ordered the college to dissolve the grammar school, but the college united in its defence, protesting to the commissioners that it was a 'nurse' to train up youth in virtue and learning, appealing to Cranmer, and receiving support from the city which itself directly petitioned the king.[10] Magdalen was now rent with factions, and a group of the younger fellows appealed to the king's council for the removal of Oglethorpe, alleging his hostility to reform and to themselves in particular. The council gladly entertained their petition, hoping to replace him by William Turner, a Cambridge radical whom it had just failed to put into the provostship of Oriel. Protector Somerset was alive to the importance of these college headships which, he reported, required 'as great care and furtherance' as nominations to bishoprics. In May 1550 Oglethorpe was summoned before the council to answer charges, but he vigorously defended himself against the dissident fellows and fortified himself with the support of the seniors. He even tried to pacify his opponents by entertaining Bucer, Peter Martyr, and Miles Coverdale in hall, but by August 1552 he had been brought to resign.[11]

Turner's candidature was an ominous sign, for unlike all those who had hitherto been recommended to the college as president, he had never been a fellow of Magdalen or New College as the statutes required. When, in 1552, the council finally decided to replace Oglethorpe, it was with Walter Haddon, a distinguished protestant scholar who had recently become master of Trinity Hall, Cambridge, but had no connections with Oxford. The fellows now faced the question of whether they could be forced to elect a non-statutable president. On 3 July 1552 the vice-president and the majority of the fellows wrote to the king representing Haddon's ineligibility under the statutes and humbly asking that they should not be forced to break their oaths. It was, they also

10. Macray, *Register*, ii. 22-6 for the commission; Bloxam, *Register*, iii. 109-113 for the question of the college school.

11. Macray, *Register*, ii. 56; Bloxam, *Register*, ii. 309-19; G. D. Duncan, 'The heads of houses and religious change in Tudor Oxford, 1547-1558', *Oxoniensia*, 45 (1980), 229-30; Cross, 'Oxford and the Tudor state', 138.

pointed out, 'a great disgracing and discomforting also to our college that no one man of our foundation could be thought meet to succeed our former president', and they besought the king 'not to coerce us by your power royal and supreme authority, but...to grant we have free election'.[12] They received no sympathy and by 14 August had agreed to elect Haddon as from Michaelmas. This was the product of strong pressure: two letters from the king and a special mandate dispensing from the statutory requirements and forbidding the election of any other person. Haddon was an honourable man who acted with generosity towards Oglethorpe, permitting him to remain awhile in college and undertaking to procure his reconciliation with the council. But his reign as president was destined to be short. In July 1553 Edward VI died and was succeeded by Mary; in October the catholic Stephen Gardiner, now restored to the bishopric of Winchester of which he had been deprived in 1551, conducted a visitation of the college and Haddon was ejected.[13] Oglethorpe was re-elected and quickly earned his reward from the new regime: he became dean of Windsor in 1554 and registrar of the Order of the Garter in 1555, by which time he had resigned the presidency. His rise was to culminate in appointment to the see of Carlisle in 1556 before it was cut short by the accession of Elizabeth. Although he was persuaded to crown the new queen when the other bishops had refused, he declined to accept the restored royal supremacy and was deprived of his see. Shortly afterwards he died.[14]

Oglethorpe was replaced as president by another old Henrician in the same mould: on 22 April 1555 Arthur Cole, formerly cross bearer to Wolsey and a canon of Windsor since 1543, was elected by the now predominantly catholic fellows, only to die on 18 July 1558.[15] Once again the crown signalled its 'special desire and care to have wise, grave and virtuous men placed in the room of heads of such houses', and recommended

12. Magdalen College Archives, Register E, fos. 43, 96; Duncan, 'Heads of houses', 230; Macray, *Register*, vii. 114-15.

13. Magdalen College Archives, Register E, fo. 51; Macray, *Register*, ii. 58; Bloxam, *Register*, iii. pp. xliv-lv.

14. Macray, *Register*, ii. 55-62.

15. Macray, *Register*, i. 164-5; A. B. Emden, *A Biographical Register of the University of Oxford, 1501-1540* (Oxford, 1974), 128 (hereafter cited as *BRUO, 1501-40*).

three of the fellows for consideration. But in the last weeks of Mary's reign the crown lacked the incentive and authority to influence the choice of a successor, and well before the royal letters were received the fellows had elected Thomas Coveney, bursar and principal of Magdalen Hall.[16] Within four months the crown had passed to Elizabeth.

At the time of her accession Magdalen, like the university as a whole, was essentially catholic, but alone among the colleges it had seen nine of its protestant fellows flee to the continent as a result of Gardiner's visitation in 1553. These were now restored, and though the queen's policy was to proceed gently and gradually, with a conservative reform by a new commission in 1559, it was not long before Magdalen began to emerge as a hotbed of puritanism. In September 1561 the Visitor, Bishop Horne, conducted his own visitation and, finding that Coveney was 'an enemy to the sincere religion of Christ' and unacceptable to the younger fellows, some of whom he had expelled, deprived him. The queen conveniently professed her inability to entertain Coveney's appeal against the Visitor's jurisdiction and ordered a new election. The fellows chose Lawrence Humphrey, a considerable scholar of Calvinist sympathies, 'the only Marian exile of significance in Elizabethan Oxford', who had been made professor of divinity in the previous year. This time the crown had not needed to intervene; the Visitor had done so effectively, and though Humphrey was probably rather too militant for Elizabeth's taste, the presidency at least obviated the need for his further advancement within the church.[17]

Indeed disquiet was soon aroused at Canterbury by reports that Humphrey and the dean of Christ Church, Thomas Sampson, were refusing to wear surplices, and Archbishop Parker, with the backing of the council, initiated proceedings to bring them to book. Both men proclaimed their conscientious objection to vestments, Humphrey actually appealing to the

16. Duncan, 'Heads of houses', 233; Macray, *Register*, ii. 91-3; *BRUO, 1501-40*, 381-2, 519-20, 528.

17. C. M. Dent, *Protestant Reformers in Elizabethan Oxford* (Oxford, 1983), 11, 18-19, 23-8; Duncan, 'Heads of houses', 233; Macray, *Register*, ii. 99-100; Bloxam, *Register*, iv, 104-32; Penry Williams, 'Elizabethan Oxford; church, state, and university', in *The History of the University of Oxford*, iii. 405-6.

queen herself. He was imprisoned briefly for disobedience and on release discreetly withdrew to the country. But whereas Parker could, and did, deprive Sampson for disobedience, he could not touch Humphrey who was subject only to the jurisdiction of the Visitor. As he pointed out, 'both Magdalens [i.e. in Oxford and Cambridge] are out of the university; both separate and exempt places'. In any case there were too few of Humphrey's intellectual status in the university for him to be easily sacrificed, and he escaped with a memorable royal rebuke. When the queen visited the university at the end of August 1566 and was received by Humphrey in his scarlet robes, she remarked as he kissed her hand, 'Methinks that loose gown becomes you mighty well; I wonder your notions be so strait laced — but I come not now to chide'.[18] Bishop Horne's visitation of the college which immediately followed left Humphrey's position unscathed, though he strictly enforced the use of surplices. Humphrey, who had an eye to his own advancement, learned to conform, to such good effect that he became dean of Gloucester and eventually of Winchester, and served as vice-chancellor of the university (1572-6). Gradually he assumed the role of an elder statesman, while some of the more 'precise', i.e. puritan, fellows found themselves increasingly opposed to his government. In 1575 the crisis was precipitated when Humphrey expelled six of those who opposed his authority on a point of discipline. Though the Visitor upheld the president, the affair quickly gained notoriety, drawing in others from outside, and even alarming Walsingham and the council, always alert to the danger of divisions within the established church. Nor were the disputes within the college easily healed; they broke out again in 1578 and 1581, and by 1585 the new bishop of Winchester, Thomas Cooper, was forced to undertake a full visitation. A dossier of complaints was presented against Humphrey's failure to enforce 'godly religion', his lax discipline, and mismanagement of the finances; but the president's health was already failing and he died on 1 February 1589.[19]

Not surprisingly, the crown showed an active interest in the

18. C. M. Dent, *Protestant Reformers*, 33-9; Williams, 'Elizabethan Oxford', 418.

19. The whole episode is related in Dent, *Protestant Reformers*, 47-68.

choice of a successor. Within days of Humphrey's death the college received a signet letter from the queen expressing 'the special care we have of the state of that House to be preserved by good order and government of a wise and learned man' and specially recommending to them Dr Nicholas Bond as 'likely to repair and reform the late decays and disorders thereof'. To leave the fellows in no doubt the queen proceeded: 'we will and command you, and every of you, immediately upon the receipt hereof ... to nominate and elect unto the place of your President the said Dr Bond'. Bond was a chaplain in ordinary to the queen; he had been dean, bursar, and vice-president of the college in the previous decade, and was undoubtedly well qualified. Nevertheless there was opposition from the radical puritan wing, which feared that he would only perpetuate Humphrey's regime, and these seem to have been joined by others who resented royal interference. Led by John Harding, they nominated one Ralph Smith, a fellow since 1568, though he had never held college office, and had recently resigned to accept the living of Milton Keynes. At the first scrutiny he may well have secured a majority of the votes among all the fellows, for as the nomination papers were being prepared for the final choice by the thirteen seniors, one of Bond's supporters, fearing his defeat, seized the nominating slips and tore them up. Smith's supporters then wrote his name on odd pieces of paper and threw them on to the communion table, while those supporting Bond left the chapel. The Smithites claimed that eight votes had been cast for their man, who thus had a majority, but Bond's men had rendered the election invalid through these disorders and ensured that it could not be completed within the seventeen days prescribed by statute. Both parties sought to justify their actions. On 21 February twelve of Smith's supporters wrote to the archbishop of Canterbury explaining their disobedience to the queen's command on the ground that they were bound by their consciences and oaths to vote for 'him with those qualities which our Founder requireth', accusing Bond of 'lightness in behaviour and small skill or care of matters in our House'. They secured legal opinion to the effect that, although the final scrutiny had been omitted, everything of substance had been performed for a valid election. Those who voted for Bond, on the other hand, did so in strict obedience to her Majesty's prerogative 'which we take to have authority above all local statutes, and that Her Majesty may command anything contrary to our statutes', a doctrine which was to be bitterly contested in 1687. His supporters stressed that, since Bond was statutorily eligible, disobedience to the queen would incur her 'insupportable indignation against our society' and encourage the pretensions of 'the precise sort' in the university. Elizabeth had the last word. Claiming that the proceedings had been irregular and invalid, and that the nomination had thereby reverted to the crown, she annulled the election of Smith and 'by her own motion' appointed Bond by letter patent on 5 April.[20]

The sixty years since Henry VIII's break with Rome had thus seen a fairly continuous record of intervention in the elections to the presidency. Only two seem to have proceeded without pressure of some kind on the fellows, those of Arthur Cole in 1555 and of William Coveney in 1558, and in the second of these the crown had made its wishes known, though too late to affect the election. On all but two occasions those recommended to the fellows had been technically eligible under the statutes, though objections were raised to the character of some. On the two occasions when non-statutable outsiders had been proposed, the college had successfully objected to William Turner in 1550 but had bowed to the mandate to elect Walter Haddon in 1552. As a whole the college was ready to resist breaches of its statutes and to recognise the propriety of recommendations, but it was divided in its attitude to royal mandates ordering the election of a named candidate under the threat of royal displeasure. Many accepted the royal view that Magdalen's preeminence put it in the same category as bishoprics and that its fellows should expect to be treated like a cathedral chapter and told to elect the crown's nominee. Others — usually the minority — claimed liberty of conscience to elect freely under the guidance of the Holy Spirit. The two viewpoints, conforming to those of Anglicans and Puritans within the church, were articulated in the Bond-Smith disputed

20. Dent, op. cit., 68-73; Macray, *Register*, ii. 171-82 (Bond), 186-7 (Smith); Magdalen College Archives, Register G, fo. 279v; Wilson, *Magdalen College*, 133-4; Williams, 'Elizabethan Oxford', 421.

election, the only occasion when the crown directly intervened to appoint a president notwithstanding the statutes. Two presidents had been forcibly ejected by the Visitor for their religious beliefs, Haddon in 1553 and Coveney in 1561, and Humphrey had come near to being so, while two others were persuaded to resign under pressure from the council, Knolles in 1536 and Oglethorpe in 1552. As an influential seminary which had become a battleground between radical and conservative forces in a period of violent religious change, Magdalen could not hope to escape intervention in its affairs. Yet until the election of Bond in 1589 none of the presidents in this phase of its history was a close servant of the crown and none stood so high in the royal favour as had Mayew at the beginning of the century. In the crown's eyes Magdalen had become a troublesome college, which needed to be controlled but did not deserve to be specially favoured.

The last years of Elizabeth's reign brought a steady improvement in the relations between the crown and the college. Elizabeth had confidence in Bond, not least for his ability to keep the puritan element under control, and he did much to strengthen ties with the court. On the occasion of the queen's visit to Oxford in 1592 her courtiers were feasted in the college hall. Another manifestation of this was the increasing frequency of royal recommendations for fellowships. In May 1577 Elizabeth sent letters requiring the fellows to elect John Everie, the son of one of her sergeants at arms, and when a year later his admission to actuality was opposed by a number of the fellows, the Visitor intervened to reprimand them for their 'uncomlie carelessness of the Queen Majesty's letters' and to expel the dissidents. In the following year William Sterill was elected to a fellowship. Suspect among the fellows for his Romish leanings, these were in fact a cover for his work as a secret agent of the crown to keep recusants and Jesuits under surveillance. A more agreeable, if more feckless, beneficiary of royal favour was Samuel Foxe, the son of the martyrologist, whom President Humphrey had to expel for misbehaviour but who was restored to his fellowship by royal mandate in 1581 on the appeal of his father. The queen's letters were again received in 1583 on behalf of Paul Browne, in response to his own petition pleading poverty; he also persuaded the chancellor, the earl of Leicester, to write on his behalf. He proved a contentious character. Punished in the following years for scandalous speaking, for blowing out the candles at a disputation, and for occasional absences, he was yet able to secure further royal letters in 1589 appointing him to a praelectorship in law, on the ground that he was 'more meete for the study of cyvill law than of divinite'. Finally in 1602 there was considerable pressure from the court to elect Edward Othen to a fellowship, and when not he but John Burrows was chosen by a majority of the fellows, President Bond deemed it prudent to write to the lord treasurer to explain the circumstances and absolve himself. He had, he said, read the letters of recommendation to the fellows, and as it became clear that they were minded to defy these, he had withdrawn. There was some talk of prosecuting the college, but in the last days of the old regime nothing was done and it was left to James I to procure Othen the post of praelector in natural philosophy in 1605.[21]

Just how far the college was now esteemed to be the particular recipient of royal favour in Oxford was made clear by the first of the Stuarts. Within two years of his accession James I brought his queen and eldest son to Oxford. They were entertained in hall, and on 28 August 1605 Prince Henry was formally matriculated into Magdalen College and assigned rooms and a tutor. He declared that it was 'his college' and promised to take care for its future well being. The king himself visited the college, attended a disputation, displayed his learning while examining the library, and emphasised his beneficence by avowing that the college would find it 'a second foundation to you'.[22] The king naturally expected that his favour would be reciprocated by dutiful obedience, and when President Bond died in 1608 he busied himself with paternalistic care in the choice of a successor. Having consulted Archbishop Bancroft and the chancellor, the earl of Dorset, James saw fit to recommend his chaplain, John Harding, Regius Professor of Hebrew in the university, requiring the fellows to elect him 'in such sort as to your duty appertaineth'. The king's letter of 10 February was followed two days later by one from

21. Wilson, *Magdalen College*, 124; Macray, *Register*, iii. 64-5, 88-90; Bloxam, *Register*, iv. 204, 235-8; Williams, 'Elizabethan Oxford', 434-5.
22. Macray, *Register*, iii. 37-8, 118.

the earl of Dorset admonishing them to have 'due regard to His Majesty's recommendation' and to give 'no occasion to His Majesty by any your causeless opposition to censure your undutifulness or indiscretion'. Evidently reports had reached the chancellor that the fellows were not wholly compliant. Harding was an opinionated and erratic man, who had himself led the opposition to Bond's election. As this resistance became known, a veritable broadside followed from Dorset and Bancroft, aimed at the vice-president, John Pusey, who was the internal candidate. Pusey's candidature was stigmatised as 'tasting of arrogance and presumption in respect of his own mean parts and the eminence of that place'; his supporters were accused of allowing 'faction and humour to prevail more than duty and reason'; their protests against the royal mandate were deemed to 'cast some aspersion upon His Majesty and us of his Highness Council, as if your local statutes were violated and your liberties infringed ... which imputation as it highly offendeth his Highness ... you are to be taught to know that under pretext of a free election you must not have licence to abuse your Founder's good purpose and intention'. Pusey and his supporters were summoned before the council. On receipt of this letter they capitulated, 'prostrating ourselves before his excellent Majesty and the rest of his honourable council' and averring their innocence of 'any complotting in factious manner'. At the election three days later Harding had the majority, but his reign lasted less than three years and on his death in November 1610 the college faced another election.[23]

This time all parties seem to have been anxious to avoid the embarrassments of Harding's election. The court candidate was William Langton, an able scholar who had disputed at the king's visit in 1605, becoming chaplain to Robert Cecil, earl of Salisbury, who was said to have procured commendatory letters from the king to the fellows for Langton's election. There is no record of these, and according to the sermon preached at his death, Langton 'would not so distrust the love of the fellows, or wrong the freedom of their voices and consciences, as to use them; and therefore kept them still sealed up until, by the freest way of unconstrained voices, he was chosen'. Yet there was

23. Ibid. iii. 73-9.

strong opposition among the puritan fellows, and he did not gain an overall majority of votes on the first scrutiny. Court pressure was certainly instrumental in his election.[24] During the sixteen years of Langton's presidency harmonious relations were maintained with the crown, even though the death of Prince Henry in 1612 disappointed the extravagant expectations raised by the visit of 1605. James and his court frequently passed through Oxford on his way to Woodstock, and the college dutifully saluted his progress with trumpeters; but the king himself never again entered its doors.

Although the college could not claim James I's heir and successor as one of its members as it had hoped, it quickly established a personal link with Charles I through its next president. For when Langton died on 10 October 1626 a candidate was in place eminently qualified by his learning, reputation in the college, and acceptability to the court. Accepted Frewen, praelector in philosophy and vice-president, had been chaplain at the embassy in Madrid during the visit of Prince Charles and the duke of Buckingham to woo the Spanish Infanta. His sermon before the prince on the text 'How long halt ye between two opinions' (1 Kings xviii, 21) had made a lasting impression on Charles, who appointed him his chaplain. He was elected president on 24 October. Even at that date the puritan candidate, William Sparkes, who had also stood against Langton, received 29 votes at the first scrutiny, but this was the last stand of the puritan faction and under the new president the religious complexion of the college was utterly changed. Frewen had been raised as a puritan, but he now adopted the principles of Laudianism which were sweeping the university. Laud became chancellor in April 1629 and Frewen's career advanced under the shadow of Laud, whom he succeeded as dean of Gloucester in 1631, serving as his vice-chancellor in 1629 and 1638-9. The furnishings and services of the college chapel were transformed. When the civil war came the college's loyalty to Charles I followed that of its head. On 6 January 1643 the king wrote to the president and fellows asking them to 'lend unto us all such plate of what kind so ever belongs to your college', trusting in their 'readiness and affection to assist your

24. Ibid. iii. 112-3.

king in such visible necessity'. The college delivered 220 lb of silver plate and 66 lb of gilt. No other college sent as much for the king's cause, and Magdalen added a loan in cash of £1,000, half of it from the president himself. Frewen's loyalty was not forgotten; next year he was consecrated bishop of Coventry and Lichfield in the college chapel, and eventually at the Restoration was elevated to the see of York.[25]

He resigned the presidency on 11 May 1644 and his successor, John Oliver, was elected on 28 May. Oliver was Laud's domestic chaplain, and there is no need to look further for the influence behind his election. But it only just preceded the collapse of the royalist position. Oxford capitulated to Fairfax's army in 1646, and by March 1648 a parliamentary commission had removed Oliver, along with other heads of houses.[26] By parliamentary authority John Wilkinson was appointed president in his place and all members of the foundation were required to profess submission to the commissioners and obedience to the new president. Many refused, objecting that Wilkinson had been neither elected nor admitted in conformity with the statutes. They were in consequence ejected.[27] This was Wilkinson's revenge for his own removal by Charles I in 1643 from the office of principal of Magdalen Hall which he had ruled for forty years, fostering Calvinist opinions. He was a narrow, ill-tempered man whose presidency is remembered for the dispersal of the store of gold sovereigns ('spur royals') bequeathed by Waynflete to sustain the college in emergencies. He died on 6 January 1650, but before the fellows could meet to elect a successor parliament had itself appointed Thomas Goodwin, on 8 January. Goodwin had never been a fellow of the college; he was a Cambridge man, a well-known Independent, and a prolific writer. Addison satirised his godly and eccentric rule of the college by recounting how a young candidate, seeking admission, found himself interviewed by the president swathed in a head dress against the cold, with religious terror in his face, who examined him not on his Latin and Greek but on the nature of his

25. On Frewen, Bloxam, *Register*, v. 10-20; Wilson, *Magdalen College*, 152.
26. Bloxam, *Register*, v. 82-8; Macray, *Register*, iii. 155-6; Wilson, *Magdalen College*, 155-8.
27. Macray, *Register*, iii. 117-21; Wilson, *Magdalen College*, 161-6.

conversion, whether he was of the elect, and how he was preparing for death. Independent meetings were held at the Lodgings where all openly confessed their sins. Eventually, on 9 May 1660, shortly before the return of the Stuarts, he resigned.[28] Once again the fellows were prevented from electing a successor, for the House of Lords ordered the restoration of John Oliver along with the fellows expelled in 1648. Thus on three successive occasions the appointment to the presidency had been made by parliamentary authority, and on one of these the person had been statutorily ineligible. Indeed the power of parliament to annul the Founder's statutes had earlier been demonstrated by the abolition of the restriction of fellowships to those from particular counties.

An uneasy calm endured in the college until the death of Oliver on 27 October 1661. The Presbyterians and Independents who had acquired fellowships under the previous regime were not expelled, but the college expected to resume its favoured relationship with the house of Stuart, and Charles II soon showed that he looked for dutiful obedience to his wishes. On 1 November 1661 he wrote recommending for election as president Thomas Pierce, praelector in theology, his chaplain in ordinary, and a recent preacher before both houses of parliament. The king's letter declared his 'expectation and will that you choose him for your president and that you suffer him not to be prejudiced by any competition whatsoever in his pretence to a place'. But some of the fellows, probably dissenters, were minded to show their independence by canvassing for John Tayleur. When this reached the king's ears a further letter, a week later, reprimanded them and strictly enjoined the fellows 'not to fail to choose for your future president the said Dr Pierce, or you shall know what it is to disrespect your king'. Two days later Pierce was unanimously elected.[29] An accomplished musician and poet, the friend of Peter Heylin, Pierce was also an indefatigable controversialist and proved something of a disaster, stirring up trouble and opposition by his sharp tongue and ill-tempered actions. Eventually on 4 March 1672 he resigned.

28. Macray, *Register*, vii, 115-6; Bloxam, *Register*, ii. pp. cix-cxi.
29. Bloxam, *Register*, v. 168-70; Wilson, *Magdalen College*, 179.

The last presidential election before that of 1687 had some unusual and significant features. For Pierce only agreed to resign if he could nominate as his successor Dr Henry Clerke — who, it was rumoured, had paid him handsomely for the service. To achieve this Pierce secured a letter from the king dated 27 February recommending Clerke as well qualified under the statutes and by his long occupancy of college offices — he had indeed been a fellow since 1642, three times bursar, and twice vice-president. He was also, most unusually, a doctor of medicine and lecturer in anatomy, who only took holy orders on his election to the presidency. Although the king's letters did not 'will and require' the fellows to elect Clerke, their ready compliance was anticipated and they were reminded of the king's gracious care for their society. The letter was endorsed by Arlington, as secretary of state. Clerke himself had no access to the court; the king's intervention was rather a favour to Pierce, and it followed a trend that had been increasing in elections to fellowships.[30] Significantly the procedure at Clerke's election likewise followed that which had become usual for fellows elected on royal mandates. This avoided the scrutiny of written nominations and votes and proceeded by oral nomination, which dispensed with an oath to uphold the statutes, and allowed many fellows to qualify their assent by stating that they gave it in obedience to the king's command.

Just how habitual royal intervention in elections to fellowships had become is difficult to gauge. All the Stuarts practised it, but it occurred with increasing frequency under Charles II. In 1668 there were no less than three royal interventions, and one of these, in favour of John Chambers, reveals the same process of nominating a successor as in the election of Clerke. Simon Bradley, elected a fellow in 1662 and now a royal chaplain, agreed to resign in favour of Chambers, doubtless for a consideration, and applied to Arlington for a royal letter in favour of Chambers. He cited five previous examples of the practice, though admitting that only at New College and All Souls were royal mandates accepted. The king's letter, dated 18 March, recited Bradley's petition and Charles II's pleasure that 'forthwith on the receipt of these our letters

30. Bloxam, *Register*, v. 154-6.

we will and require you to admit and elect' Chambers.[31] The extent to which royal authority was being manipulated by place seekers at court was revealed when, later in the same year, the college received in April one royal letter, again endorsed by Arlington, requiring the election of Samuel Russell to a vacant fellowship, to be followed in July by another requiring the election of Grandisson Turner to the same. When the fellows assembled for the election the president revealed the quandary. Some wanted to go ahead and choose according to their conscience, but President Pierce urged the postponement of the election until he could contact the court and ascertain whom the king preferred. This he did and Charles indicated that Russell should be elected; he had forgotten that he had already written for him when Turner presented his own petition.[32] Fellowships were thus becoming the common coin of royal favour, and viewed, like court and government offices, as freeholds to be negotiated by private treaty. When this extended to the presidency itself, as it did with Clerke's election, it signified a fundamental shift from the era of the Tudors.

With the Reformation the crown had begun to exert its authority over the office of president as a means of religious and political control, choosing men whom it could trust for their obedience and conformity. Under the early Stuarts royal authority continued to be directly exercised, but with political loyalty less an issue the presidency again became a reward for favoured court chaplains. Under the Commonwealth and Protectorate, parliament asserted its authority to override college statutes, and the college was plunged back into the religious factionalism of the mid-sixteenth century. Only with the Stuart restoration under a pragmatic and mercenary king did the era of religio-political conviction which had begun with the Reformation appear to have finally ended, and the era of patronage politics to have begun. In this perspective the events of 1687-8 came as an unlooked-for throw-back to another age.

As this survey has shown, the tradition of royal intervention in the affairs of the college, and notably in the choice of the president, was almost as old as the college itself. But though

31. Macray, *Register*, iv. 114-6.
32. Ibid. iv. 117; Bloxam, *Register*, v. 259-62.

anticipated as a matter of course, it conformed to certain presumptions and guidelines.

1. Magdalen College was acknowledged to enjoy some kind of special relationship with the crown, expressed in the king's concern and care for the well being of the college in general and the extension of royal favour to the president and some individual fellows.

2. On a vacancy in the presidency royal mandates would normally be received recommending the name of a successor, and though they might be worded with varying degrees of stringency, the crown expected them to be obeyed, and could be confident that, in the end, the royal nominee would be elected.

3. Nevertheless this was so only with two qualifications:

   a) there was often opposition to the crown's nomination from a group of fellows asserting conscientious obedience to their statutory oath to choose freely under the guidance of the Holy Spirit. Although this served to keep alive the principle of freedom of conscience, in most cases the opposition came from a religious-political faction in the college;

   b) the fellows would always unite to resist the nomination of a non-statutable outsider, i.e. one who had not previously been a fellow of the college, as in the cases of Turner, Haddon, and Goodwin.

4. Whether and in what circumstances the college statutes governing the election of a president could be set aside was not wholly clear. The precedents accumulated over the previous two centuries were as follows. The crown itself had never intruded a nominee without first recommending a name for due election, and Elizabeth's exercise of royal authority to appoint Bond had been justified on the ground that the conduct of the election had been irregular. At Bond's election the royal party within the college appears to have claimed that the prerogative had authority above all local statutes and that the queen could command anything contrary to the statutes. Certainly Edward VI had dispensed the fellows from obedience to the statutes in requiring them to elect Walter Haddon. The Stuarts took a less overtly autocratic line, priding themselves on observing the law and looking for obedience to their wishes in virtue of their divine right and the love and respect which subjects should render to a just ruler. It was parliament, rather than the crown,

which had overridden the college statutes to impose Wilkinson, Goodwin and, technically, Oliver (1660). The Visitor, for his part, undoubtedly had a right to refuse to confirm an election, as Foxe had in the case of Veysey, and he could also deprive an incumbent president for good cause. The crown itself had never deprived a president, though it had brought pressure on Knolles and Oglethorpe to resign.

5. Over the previous two centuries the presidency had been held by men with highly diverse religious views, from Roman Catholics to Independents, in conformity with the prevailing complexion of the government. But after the Restoration in 1660 there was some expectation that the era of religio-political strife which had begun in the 1530s had passed, and that both the Anglican church and the two universities could expect to remain undisturbed from further doctrinal intervention. Magdalen, indeed, was showing signs of integrating itself happily into the crown's patronage network and developing the comfortable and mercenary view that its fellowships were freeholds which could be rendered a marketable commodity through a willingness to allow the crown an effective right of nomination. Corruption had even begun to embrace the presidency itself, when the events of 1687-8 showed that those who played with the fire of royal prerogative might themselves get burnt.

It is hazardous to define the character of a college at so remote a stage in its history, yet the impression remains that Magdalen was a society difficult to govern from within and unpredictable in its response to the world outside. As a wealthy, large, and influential college, it drew upon itself the attention of the powers in both church and state, and it numbered among its fellows men whose abilities and ambitions could not be confined within its walls. Some were eager for patronage, anxious to display their loyalty, and conformable to the wishes of the crown. Others were resistant, whether from principle, personal distaste, or factious opposition. But all alike felt assured of the college's preeminence and cherished the independence afforded by its statutes. Thus while the fellows laid claim to special favours and a special status, in the eyes of the crown Magdalen too often appeared a loyal but also a troublesome college.

THE COLLEGE, KING JAMES II
AND THE REVOLUTION
1687-1688

*

ANGUS MACINTYRE

On Sunday 4 September 1687 at three o'clock in the afternoon, the fellows of Magdalen were ordered to appear before King James II in the Dean's Lodgings in Christ Church where the king was staying. Twenty-one appeared, led by Dr Alexander Pudsey, the bursar and the senior fellow then in the college. As the fellows knelt before him, the king, whose face changed colour as his anger 'prevented him from continuing his speech for some moments', upbraided them in the severest terms for their persistent disobedience:

> You have been a stubborn, turbulent College, I have known you to be so these 6 & twenty years my self. You have affronted me; Is this y^r Church of England loyalty? One would wond^r to see so many Church of England men gott togeth^r in such a business. Go back & shew your selves good members of ye Church of England, Get you gon, Know I am y^r King; & y^t I com̄and you to be gon, Go & admitt ye Bp of Oxford Head, Principall, or w^t do you call it, of y^r College (one y^t stood by said President) I mean President of y^r Coll. ... or else you must expect to feel ye heavy hand of an angry King.[1]

After this combined order and threat had been repeated and after James had brusquely refused to receive a petition setting

---

1. Magdalen College Archives MS 421, fo.5: Henry Holden to William Holden, 18 Sept. 1687. Holden had particular reason for exactly recalling James's words since the king went on furiously to ask why Holden's election as a fellow had been confirmed after the arrival of the royal mandate which, in James's view, implied an inhibition on all the college's proceedings. The fellows' answer that this was the 'consummation' of a previous election was described by James as 'a fresh aggravation'. Holden's version of James's speech

out the college's case, the fellows withdrew. Meeting in the chapel later that afternoon, nineteen of those who had appeared before the king refused to comply with his command. Their conduct did indeed show their 'Church of England loyalty': in that much at least, James was unwittingly right. But it also showed much else besides. The case of Magdalen College was by this time an issue of national importance.

Why did a thoroughly loyal and tory college which had suffered for its loyalty during the Commonwealth and had been consistently faithful to the royalist cause, now refuse to obey its king? What were the consequences of this disobedience not only for the college but also for the stability of the king's regime? We lack a relatively detailed, modern account of this momentous episode in the history of the college: the tercentenary of the 'Restoration' of the college, coinciding with that of the Revolution of 1688, is a proper occasion to provide one. The struggle between James II and Magdalen has not of course been neglected by historians. Hume, wondering philosophically at James's 'infatuation' in pursuing his Catholic policies and finding this surprising in a man 'not deficient in sense and accomplishments', concluded in 1757 that James's 'act of violence' against Magdalen was 'perhaps the most openly illegal and arbitrary' of his reign.[2] A century later, Macaulay devoted some of the most memorable and eloquent passages in his *History* to the case. For him, the expulsion of the president, fellows and demies and the conversion of the college into 'a Popish seminary' 'dissolved those ties, once so close and dear, which had bound the Church of England to the House of Stuart', even if it had not yet driven

agrees with only minor differences with that in *An Impartial Relation of the whole Proceedings against St Mary Magdalen Colledge in Oxon, in the year of our Lord 1687, containing only Matters of Fact as they Occurred* (1688), 15-16, the college's unacknowledged but official account published early in 1688 and put together probably by the vice-president Charles Aldworth, who had the assistance of Robert Almont, fellow and bursar in 1688: see MS drafts of part of the *Impartial Relation* in Magdalen College MS 908/26, Appleton Papers, (Almont's papers). Other versions of James's confrontation with the fellows, all broadly consistent with each other, are in *Magdalen College and King James II, 1686-1688*, ed. J. R. Bloxam (Oxford, 1886), 84-7 (hereafter *Magdalen and James*).

2. David Hume, *History of Great Britain: The Commonwealth, and the Reigns of Charles II and James II* (London, 1757)', ii. 412, 408.

the tories from their attitude of non-resistance to an unjust ruler.[3] Yet these and other accounts by recent historians of James II's reign naturally treat the episode as part of a broader, formal narrative with relatively slight reference to themes and personalities of interest in the college's history or to the remarkable, often painful, occasionally comic private dramas of those most closely concerned. From these 'college' and human viewpoints the story has not been re-told since 1899 when H. A. Wilson published his history of the college.[4] Like all other accounts, including this one, Wilson owes and acknowledges a great debt to the collection of documents assembled largely by a Victorian fellow, the Rev. J. R. Bloxam, and published as *Magdalen College and King James II* in 1886. That volume is even scarcer than Wilson's history.

By the beginning of James II's reign in 1685, the two ancient English universities and their constituent colleges had been firmly re-established as pillars of the political and social order. Oxford in particular was the stronghold of monopolistic Anglican orthodoxy and fervent loyalism. The university had proclaimed in 1683 its official support for divine right monarchy and the subject's duty of 'passive obedience' to any ruler, even an unjust one; it had condemned and burnt books such as those of Milton and Hobbes which contained 'Damnable Doctrines Destructive to the Sacred Persons of Princes'.[5] Oxford fêted James on his visit as duke of York in 1683, when his duchess was pleased to be received in Magdalen with an oration in Italian from Dr John Younger; and James's coronation was celebrated with jubilant ceremonies, bonfires and 'Great extraordinaries in eating and drinking in each College'.[6] In 1685, the university gave active support to the

---

3. Lord Macaulay, *The History of England from the Accession of James II* (London, 1931 edn.), ii. 263, 264.

4. H. A. Wilson, *Magdalen College* (London, 1899), ch. xiv.

5. G. V. Bennett, 'Loyalist Oxford and the Revolution', *The History of the University of Oxford: vol. v: The Eighteenth Century*, ed. L. S. Sutherland and L. G. Mitchell (Oxford, 1986), 11.

6. *The Life and Times of Anthony Wood, antiquary, of Oxford, 1632-1695*, ed. Andrew Clark (Oxford, 1894), iii. 141 (23 April 1685).

suppression of Monmouth's rebellion: Magdalen with other colleges raised companies, and the college's contingent, which never saw action, was commanded by Captain Francis Bagshaw, one of the fellows.[7] Like the vast majority of dons, the fellows of Magdalen were, in the late G. V. Bennett's authoritative words, 'guardians of a body of traditional learning on which religious orthodoxy, political obedience and social order were thought to depend'.[8] Aided by its considerable wealth and comparatively large size, the college was efficiently performing its public tasks as a religious and educational foundation: the provision of large numbers of soundly-trained clergymen whose religious duties in the parishes were bound up with social and political influence, and the education of the sons of the nobility and gentry, and to a diminishing but still significant extent, of yeomen and humbler families. The large fellowship (forty by the college's statutes) was respectable in general quality and contained some men of real distinction. Magdalen was a powerful force in university affairs, and nursed a traditional and keen rivalry with Christ Church — a point not to be overlooked in assessing some future events.

James II's strategy as king did not differ essentially from Charles II's in his last years. Both wanted to increase the personal power of the monarchy, to build and use a reliable 'king's party' of Anglicans, Protestant dissenters and Roman Catholics; in James's case he sought the general religious toleration which Charles had attempted earlier. They differed radically in motives and tactics: Charles was subtle, devious, whimsical as to religion, and a political realist; James, a far more open personality, candid and bluff to the point of obtuseness, more trustworthy and more inclined to trust others, was passionately devoted to his Roman faith. Uncertain of his own health and with no male heir until the birth of the Prince of Wales in June 1688, he was keenly aware that the

---

7. For these companies' exercises in Christ Church meadow and elsewhere, see Wood, *Life and Times*, iii. 146-52. The officers wore 'scarlet coats, scarfes about their wasts (*sic*), and white feathers in their hats'. Capt. Bagshaw's 'feather...was so bigg that nothing of the hat could be seen'. At one point he trained his company in the college quadrangle. Their colours were quarterly sable and argent, with three coronets or; on a canton argent a cross gules.

8. G. V. Bennett, 'University, Society and Church, 1688-1714', *History of the University of Oxford*, v. 359.

heiress-presumptive, his elder daughter Princess Mary, was a staunch Anglican and as firm in her faith as her Calvinist husband William, Prince of Orange. James had to move quickly if his policies were to take root before they might soon be undone.

His first aim was to free his co-religionists from their civil and religious disabilities, but he also believed the Roman faith to be so self-evidently true that the English people had only to hear it properly preached and freely taught to be converted as he had been. The tory and loyalist reaction of Charles II's last years increased James's self-confidence: despite signs of opposition and insubordination in his own first parliament, he thought that this Anglican loyalism was malleable and likely to be amenable to resolute manipulation. His dynamic use of his prerogative powers, notably the power to suspend statutes and to dispense individuals from statutory obligations, affected all institutions: the electoral system and parliament, the municipal corporations and county government, the church, the law courts and the armed services. The universities were particularly important in his strategy. If Catholics could be put into positions of authority in them, true Catholic doctrine would challenge Anglican heresy in its heartland and transform the religion of present and future generations. The universities, in which he thought or was persuaded to think that there were many secret Catholics, were therefore crucial in his Catholic mission in England.[9]

Rejecting implicitly any idea of founding new Catholic colleges in favour of infiltrating and re-modelling existing ones, James turned first to Cambridge. Joshua Basset, a reputed Roman, was made master of Sidney Sussex (Oliver Cromwell's college, a fact which must have given the king a certain pleasure); and for the university's refusal to admit a Benedictine monk, Father Alban Francis, as an M.A. without taking the oath of supremacy or subscribing to the Thirty-nine Articles, the vice-chancellor, Dr John Peachell, was deprived of

---

9. For James's policies, see John Miller, *Popery and Politics in England, 1660-1688* (Cambridge, 1973), and J. R. Jones, *The Revolution of 1688 in England* (London, 1972). To these valuable recent accounts should be added David Ogg, *England in the Reigns of James II and William III* (Oxford, 1969 edn.), chs. II-VII.

his office and suspended as master of Magdalene.[10] Oxford offered a more important and more promising field of operations. The influential master of University College, Obadiah Walker, had turned papist and soon started up a licensed printing press in the college to disseminate Catholic works.[11] In July 1686 the king ordered the canons of Christ Church to install as dean one of Walker's disciples, John Massey, a fellow of Merton and a Catholic. He was clearly unqualified but he was also armed like Walker with royal dispensation from Anglican religious duties, and to the indignation of good churchmen the canons spiritlessly complied with the king's order. As discipline among the undergraduates collapsed, Massey set up a Roman chapel in Canterbury quadrangle. Promising bridgeheads for the king's cause had therefore been established in Oxford when news was received of the death in Lancashire on 24 March 1687 of the aged Henry Clerke, president of Magdalen since 1672. His daughter Lady Shuttleworth, with whom he had been staying at Gawthorpe Hall, gave first notice of her father's death not to the college but to a senior fellow, the courtly John Younger, who was residing in London as chaplain to Princess Anne. He learnt the news on the 26th, the college on the 29th.

In the matter of elections to the presidency, the king could see favourable immediate precedents on his side: Charles II had nominated Thomas Pierce in 1661, although his actual election had required a royal threat as to the consequences of non-compliance; in Clerke's case many of the fellows made it clear that he was not their preferred choice and that they elected him in obedience to the king's mandate. These precedents were encouraging for James only if the reluctant and 'passively obedient' attitude of the fellows was ignored.[12] It was expected

10. V. H. H. Green, *Religion at Oxford and Cambridge. A History c.1160-c.1960* (London, 1964), 169.

11. Hence the doggerel catch, attributed to the young wits of Christ Church:
> Oh, old Obadiah,
> Sing Ave Maria,
> But so will not I a
>   for why a
> I had rather be a fool than a knave a.

Walker, aged 70 in 1687, was the leading spirit of the Catholic cause in Oxford and the king's chief local adviser on university affairs.

12. Wilson, *Magdalen College*, 179-80, 183-5. James's description of the

that James would intervene, and it was soon clear what was in his mind. Dr Thomas Smith, known as 'Rabbi' or 'Tograi' Smith, one of the more senior and certainly the most learned of the fellows, was told at once in London of Clerke's death by Younger who made it clear that he himself was not a candidate. On pressing his own claims to the presidency through Samuel Parker, bishop of Oxford, Smith was told by Parker that 'the King expected that the person he recommended should be favourable to his religion.[13] Smith, whose Anglicanism was impeccable, promptly dropped his claims. Except for his scholarship and knowledge of the world, his claims to support among the fellows cannot have been strong: three years earlier, when he made serious charges of corruption against Presidents Pierce and Clerke touched off by his failure to gain election as reader in divinity in the college, he received the support of only one fellow.

Meanwhile, at Magdalen, the vice-president, Dr Charles Aldworth, called the resident fellows to a meeting on 31 March which chose 13 April for the presidential election, being two days before the last day allowed by the statutes. These provided that twelve days were to be given for absent fellows to arrive. The fellows therefore had a fortnight for their preparatory moves.

Their next and sensible action was to ask for the advice of the college's Visitor, the bishop of Winchester, Dr Peter Mews. Mews was one of the more remarkable members of the episcopate. He had served as a captain in Charles I's army in the Civil War and was taken prisoner at Naseby. Later a leading

college as 'stubborn, turbulent' (above p. 31) referred not to the fellows' politics but to their reactions to Charles II's mandates in presidential elections and their 'constant disputes and appeals' to the Visitor on matters which produced frequent royal intervention during President Pierce's time.

13. Dr Thomas Smith's Narrative, 26, 28, March, 5 April 1687, in *Magdalen and James*, 3-4, 15. Smith's nicknames referred to his oriental interests (Tograi was an Arabic author whose poem he had edited); he was M.A. Queen's, joined the college as master of the School 1663 or 1664, fellow 1666; he spent three years (1668-71) at Constantinople as chaplain to the ambassador Sir Daniel Harvey, acquiring Greek manuscripts and a high reputation as an orientalist and as an authority on the Greek Orthodox Church; chaplain (1678-9) to the secretary of state Sir Joseph Williamson; vice-president 1682; bursar 1686, 1688 (when expelled). His Narrative and Diary are prime sources for the history of the college in 1687-8. For his life and works, see J. R. Bloxam, *Register*, iii. 182-204, and *DNB*.

royal agent employed on several hazardous missions on one of
which he narrowly escaped being hanged in Scotland, he
received deserved and rapid preferment after the Restoration: he
was made president of St John's College, Oxford, in 1667,
bishop of Bath and Wells in 1672, and bishop of Winchester in
1684. As a former vice-chancellor and as Visitor of four colleges,
he knew Oxford intimately. His loyalty to the Stuarts was
unquestionable, but so was his devotion to his church, his
political ability and his energy. This latter quality had been
displayed less than two years earlier when at the age of sixty-six
he directed the fire of the royal artillery on Monmouth's rebels
at Sedgemoor.[14] His advice to the college, received on 2 April,
was prompt and decisive: the fellows should lawfully and
exactly observe their statutes. He also put forward the name of
his client Baptist Levinz, bishop of Sodor and Man, who as a
former fellow of Magdalen was certainly qualified for election.
Levinz's first reactions were apparently encouraging but it then
transpired that he thought discretion the better part of valour.
His withdrawal was not thought honourable, and the fellows
were now confronted not merely by strong rumours of a
Catholic candidate but by a formal royal command.[15]

James's mandate to the college, a *mandamus* dated 5 April
and transmitted by Robert Spencer, earl of Sunderland, the lord
president of the council and principal secretary of state,
ordered the fellows to elect Anthony Farmer, a reputed Catholic
of whose 'piety, loyalty and learning' the king was well
satisfied and on whose behalf the king dispensed with 'any
statute, custom, or constitution' which might otherwise stand
in his way.[16] Originally a Cambridge man, Farmer had left that
place under something of a cloud after being severely
admonished by the master of his college (Trinity) for creating a
disturbance at a dancing school. He moved to Oxford and was

14. He must have been the last English bishop to take an active part in
warfare. The wound he received at Sedgemoor troubled him for the rest of his
life; the black patch in his portrait (Plate 1) covers a scar on his cheek, one of
some thirty wounds received in the course of his military career. He interceded
for the rebels' lives after Sedgemoor; *DNB*.

15. *Magdalen and James*, 13-4, 25, n.2; *DNB* (Levinz).

16. Sunderland to the vice-president and fellows, 5 April 1687, *Magdalen
and James*, 14-5; Magdalen College MS 730 (b), 11 April 1687, Vice-President's
Register 1661-1776.

found of 'a troublesome and unpeaceable humour' during his two years at Magdalen Hall (1683-5), after which he became a member of the college as an M.A.[17] In recommending him to the king, Obadiah Walker showed an almost ludicrous failure of judgement. Farmer was so lacking in suitable qualifications that by nominating him, James handed the fellows a trump card which they used skilfully in the opening exchanges. Farmer was not a fellow of either Magdalen or New College as the statutes required; moreover, rumours about his character and conduct were later discovered to be well-founded and were hardly compensated for by his membership (along with the dean of Christ Church) of the scientific society established in 1682 in the new university laboratory. As to his lack of the fellowship requirement, the king could point to previous clear breaches of this stipulation, as in the case of Edward VI's mandate in favour of President Haddon in 1552. But on the matter of personal qualifications, the college could and did refer to the statutory and perhaps idealistic requirements that the president 'must be a man of good reputation, and good life, of approved understanding, good manners and temper, discreet, provident, and circumspect both in spiritual and temporal affairs'.[18]

Knowing that the king's mandate in Farmer's favour was on its way but before receiving it on the 11th, the college again asked the Visitor for his advice. On 8 April he recommended an address to the king stating the college's case (it pointed out Farmer's incapacity and asked either to be left to elect a president according to the statutes or to be given another nomination). To accompany this address Mews had already written his own letter of remonstrance to Sunderland: he was 'confident', he wrote pointedly, that 'some who promote Mr Farmer's Interest cannot be ignorant' of his incapacity, and he emphasised the college's loyalty to the Crown on all occasions, 'as I particularly know in the greate affaire of the succession'

---

17. He was the son of John Farmer of Frolesworth, Leics.; admitted pensioner St John's College, Cambridge, 14 Aug. 1672 aged 14; scholar and B.A. Trinity 1676-7; M.A. 1680; Magdalen Hall 1683-5; admitted Magdalen College July 1685.

18. Wilson, *Magdalen College*, 97-8; *Magdalen and James*, 39. For Walker's recommendation of Farmer, see Bennett, 'Loyalist Oxford', 18.

when Sunderland himself had been prominent among those trying to exclude James from the throne.[19] In giving his immediate guidance and support to the fellows, Mews had much wider objectives than his visitatorial concern for the college. On 4 April, the day before the mandate in Farmer's favour was dispatched to the college, the king's intention of using his suspending and dispensing powers to the full was announced in his first Declaration of Indulgence. A general assault on the Anglican establishment in church and state was impending. As John Carswell has admirably pointed out, 'the intervention of Mews is the crucial evidence that an important section of the Anglican Church had decided to do battle over Magdalen' as an act of resistance to James's policy. The majority of the fellows did not need much encouragement to fall in with Mews's strategy for the election at Magdalen, but in what was likely to be a testing time for their collective courage, it was important for them to know that they had 'the connivance of higher authority in the Church'.[20]

The college's petition was duly delivered at Court on 10 April by Thomas Smith and the gallant Captain Bagshaw. It was returned four days later with the chilling verbal message from Sunderland that 'the King expects to be obeyed'. It seems almost certain, whatever Sunderland claimed then and later, that he did not inform the king at the time of this first petition; the lord chancellor Jeffreys knew nothing of it, and unlike Sunderland had no reason to dissemble about the matter.[21] If James knew nothing of the petition or Mews's letter, he would have seen the college's offence in proceeding to an election in the worst possible light. Sunderland may have thought that the fellows were bluffing or merely protesting for form's sake and that they would obey if given no alternative. If so, he was wrong.

19. Magdalen College MS 418, fo.483, Nathaniel Johnston Papers, Mews to Sunderland, 8 Apr. 1687 (copy); *Magdalen and James*, 15-6.

20. John Carswell, *The Descent on England. A Study of the English Revolution of 1688 and its European Background* (London, 1969), 91-3, who also points out the significant timing of this 'Anglican revolt'. Dijkvelt, William of Orange's special emissary, was in England and already in touch with Henry Compton, bishop of London, who had been suspended from his episcopal functions in 1686 for his defiance of James's religious policy.

21. *Magdalen and James*, 15-22, 182, Smith's Diary, 15 Nov. 1687.

The fellows had twice adjourned the election from the chosen date in order to learn the king's reaction to their petition. This was known on the 14th. On Friday 15 April, the final day for the election under the statute, the great majority of the fellows assembled in the chapel in their surplices and hoods resolved to proceed to an election. They did so against the declared advice of the vice-president and of Thomas Smith and two other senior fellows (Pudsey and Dr Henry Fairfax) to defer an election and to petition the king again. The proceedings were informal at first, with fellows moving about the chapel, and there was evidently warm debate: according to Smith, 'horrible rude reflexions were made upon the King's authority, viz. that he had nothing to do in our affair, and things of a far worse nature and consequence'. So upset was Smith that he exclaimed to one fellow that his was 'the spirit of Ferguson', the whig conspirator and Monmouth's chief adviser.[22] This was a pardonable reaction from a man of Smith's ultra-orthodox views, but quite erroneous: there was no such whiggism in Magdalen, but there plainly was passionate feeling for the college's independence and all that it now signified as well as a determination not to follow the example of Christ Church of less than a year earlier. The relative youth of the fellowship — most were in their thirties, and several were much younger — must also have been a factor: their experience for the most part was of a world apparently safe for Anglicanism and its institutions. After nearly five hours in the chapel and after the sacrament and the oaths had been administered, the final stage was reached when the thirteen most senior fellows present proceeded to vote by scrutiny. The election of the thirty-six year-old John Hough was carried by eleven votes to two, with Hough himself voting in the minority. (Two fellows, Robert Charnock, 'a declared Papist', and Jasper Thompson, a gentle-man pensioner at Whitehall, both of whom had been elected to their fellowships by James's mandate, voted separately and *viva voce* for Farmer.)[23]

No time was lost. Next day, Hough was presented by his defeated Anglican opponent Edward Maynard to the bishop of

22. Ibid. 24, Smith's Narrative, 15 April 1687.
23. Ibid. 23-30; Wilson, *Magdalen College*, 195-6.

Winchester at his palace at Farnham some 40 miles away, and was admitted at once as president. By moving so quickly they beat the king's order relayed by Sunderland on the same day to the bishop not to admit Hough, who returned to Oxford on the 17th to take the required oaths and to be installed as president at 4 o'clock prayers in the chapel. Mews told Hough and Maynard that he 'admired their courage', no mean compliment from a man of his experience.[24] That courage was soon to be tested.

John Hough (pronounced and sometimes spelt 'Huff') was in several respects unlikely material for heroism.[25] He was born in 1651 in Middlesex, the son of John Hough, a London citizen, and his wife Margaret, daughter of John Byrche of Leacroft, Staffordshire, esquire, and received his early education either at Birmingham or at Walsall; he entered Magdalen as a demy in 1669 and became an actual fellow in 1675. In 1677 he was brought to the notice of James Butler, duke of Ormonde, when Ormonde stayed in Magdalen as the guest of President Clerke. This was a stroke of luck for the young Hough in the game of patronage. Throughout a long and tempestuous career Ormonde had preserved a unique reputation as, in his biographer's words, 'an example of integrity, virtue and honour'.[26] The friend of Clarendon and the servant alike of Charles I and Charles II, chancellor of Oxford since 1669 and lord-lieutenant of Ireland from 1677 until he was relieved of his post at the beginning of James II's reign, Ormonde was the patriarch of the royalist cause. Hough served him for seven years from 1678 as his chaplain, owed his preferment in 1685 to a prebendship at Worcester to him and to royal favour, and remained faithful all his life to Ormonde's combination of firm royalism, unbending Anglicanism and essentially moderate policies. Ormonde thought equally highly of Hough, instructing his son in 1682 that if 'anybody there [in England]

24. *Magdalen and James*, 30-5.

25. For his life, see John Wilmot, *The Life of the Rev. John Hough D. D.* (London, 1812); 'Table-Talk and Papers of Bishop Hough 1703-1743', ed. W. D. Macray, *Collectanea: Second Series* (Oxford Historical Society, 1890), 383-416; *Sermons and Charges by the Right Rev. John Hough D. D.* edited with a Memoir by William Russell (Oxford, 1821); and *DNB*.

26. Thomas Carte, *An History of the Life of James, Duke of Ormonde* (London, 1736), ii. 558.

asks what religion I am of, tell them I am of Mr. Hough's religion'.[27]

Hough's character was straightforward and mild, his judgement sound, his conduct irreproachable. With no claims to scholarship, he was a conscientious and wholly orthodox churchman. If he lacked flair and imagination, these were probably useful deficiencies in his present position. He had been among the majority of the fellows determined to oppose the king's mandate and accepted his election on those terms. He was a good and generous colleague, and it may well have seemed to the fellows that his close connection with Ormonde, now residing in England, might be useful to the college. Throughout the long dispute with the king and his officials, Hough's conduct was resolute and dignified, and he also revealed an administrative ability in managing the college's case as well as his own which was the more effective for being exercised discreetly. More important, his courage and consistency held the fellows together against the many and conflicting pressures upon them.

The president and fellows immediately wrote (19 April) to Ormonde asking him to intercede on their behalf with the king, but although they remained in touch with Ormonde, there is no evidence that he was able to do anything for them. He was old, ill and almost retired from public life, and he died on 21 July 1688.[28] He and Hough, who attended him shortly before his death, must have lamented the state of affairs at Magdalen. In answer to the king's command, the college gave an account of its proceedings and sent a second address to James (23 or 24 April). The fellows could not conceive that he would have required them to act against their statutes by electing the unqualified Farmer, and they referred to the clause in those statutes by which fellows were on oath not to procure, accept or make use of any dispensation from that oath. This particular

---

27. 'Table-Talk...of Hough', 391.

28. With other governors of the Charterhouse, Ormonde had refused to comply with the king's order in December 1686 to admit a dispensed Catholic to a pensioner's place by pleading the Charterhouse's statutes. The combined influence of the governors who also included William Sancroft, archbishop of Canterbury, Henry Compton, bishop of London, and Lords Danby, Halifax and Nottingham was doubtless decisive in dissuading the king from pressing the matter.

argument against the royal dispensing power was to form a consistent element in the college's case: it was an important part of the fellows' general argument that they were bound by their statutes and by their solemn oaths to obey them. What was at stake was a conflict of jurisdictions compounded by judicial and constitutional uncertainty. The king's dispensing power had already been declared legal in the test case of *Godden v. Hales* in June 1686. Nobody — certainly not the lawyers — knew what force parliament's resolution in 1673 that penal statutes in ecclesiastical matters could only be suspended by act of parliament would have against a king determined to use his prerogative power, as James had in his Declarations of Indulgence of 4 and 27 April 1687.

James also used his powers as head of the church under the Act of Supremacy to constitute on 15 July 1686 the lords commissioners for ecclesiastical jurisdiction. To plain men, this body seemed a violation both of the Long Parliament's Act of 1641 which abolished the hated court of High Commission and of the Cavalier Parliament's confirmation of its abolition in 1662. But Stuart England contained, in David Ogg's words, 'a vast, marginal domain, where it was by no means certain what was law and what was not', and James was within his rights as to the letter of the law even if he was probably breaking its spirit and intention.[29] The ecclesiastical commission was to be James's main weapon for bringing the church of England and all educational institutions under his control. Under the Act of Supremacy, he could also look to royal powers of visitation over the universities which had been exercised in 1660 in Anglican and royalist interests against those men installed by parliament in 1648.[30] For its part, the college could appeal to its statutes

29. See Ogg, *England...James II and William III*, 175-9, for detailed argument on this issue which controverts Macaulay's view of the commission's illegality and which depends partly on the opinion that the commission was strictly not a court.

30. For these powers, see Nathaniel Johnston, *The King's Visitatorial Power asserted, being an impartial relation of the late Visitation of St. Mary Magdalen College in Oxford* (1688). Johnston (1627-1705), an able writer for the regime, author of *The Excellency of Monarchical Government* (1686), published his defence of the commissioners' visitation in reply to the college's *Impartial Relation*. His extensive notes for the work and letters to him from Obadiah Walker and Thomas Fairfax, the Jesuit fellow of Magdalen, are in Magdalen College MS 418 (Johnston Papers).

and to peculiarly binding oaths in them, to the presence of a 'local' Visitor in the bishop of Winchester, and to the freehold rights in fellowships and offices flowing from the statutes and to the laws of the land which upheld those rights. Sensibly enough, the college made rather less use of recent precedent in presidential elections.

Just over a month after the college's explanation and second address, the ecclesiastical commissioners cited the vice-president and deputed fellows on 28 May to appear before them in Whitehall. The commission included Laurence Hyde, earl of Rochester, the leading Anglican magnate (and patron of Christ Church) who was to be ousted by Sunderland from office and the king's favour; the pragmatic Nathaniel Crew, bishop of Durham; Sir Edward Herbert, lord chief justice of King's Bench; Lord Jeffreys, the lord chancellor; and Sunderland. It is a nice question who was the moving spirit of the commission: Jeffreys, who as chancellor had to act in all the commission's proceedings, or Sunderland, effectively the king's first minister.[31] Thomas Cartwright, bishop of Chester, and the judges Sir Robert Wright and Sir Thomas Jenner were later added to the commission, and all three were to play active parts in the Magdalen case.

The college's answer, signed by Aldworth as vice-president and by four of the five other deputed fellows, was delivered to the commissioners along with a copy of the statutes. When this delegation appeared before the commissioners on 13 June, Dr Henry Fairfax, who had refused to sign the answer, flatly questioned the commission's authority. Although he was the senior fellow, the stance he took was purely personal. The 'grave Doctor', as Macaulay calls him, was a member of the important Yorkshire family which produced his cousin Sir Thomas, 3rd baron Fairfax, after Cromwell the ablest of parliament's generals, and his uncle Ferdinando, 2nd baron, also a general in parliament's service; his father Charles, later an antiquary of some note, had served in the army of the

---

31. For a defence of Jeffreys as 'the incorruptible champion of royal power', see G. W. Keeton, *Lord Chancellor Jeffreys and the Stuart Cause* (London, 1965), esp. 408-9, 419-29, where it is also argued that Jeffreys did not play a prominent part in the commission and was not enthusiastic in attacking Magdalen.

Commonwealth. His family was both staunchly parliamentarian and prominent. Socially superior to most of his colleagues, he had a reputation for 'northern' bluntness of speech and humour.[32] There is no evidence that he held whiggish political views: indeed, he had been among those who advised deferring the presidential election in April. Yet it was quite consistent with the traditions of his family that he should have flouted the authority of this new Stuart commission. This he proceeded to do in a remarkable dialogue (hitherto unpublished) with the lord chancellor, who thought at first that Fairfax might be going to submit and who was not accustomed to defendants who stood up to him. Fairfax began by asking to be heard on the grounds that he was 'as good a Delegate as any of [his colleagues]', and requesting a copy of the complaint against the college in accordance with a statute of Henry V's reign (2. Henr. V. c. 3) providing for such a procedure in ecclesiastical courts. He then infuriated Jeffreys by demanding their lordships' commission and authority:

Ld. Ch.:	You are a fine Delegate indeed!
Dr. F. :	Yes my L^d, a fine Delegate...
Ld. Ch.:	You should have been kept in ye Coll. or brought to me in ye Chancery, as a Lunatiq befor you came hither; The room is too light for you, you are mad; why did they bring you out of yr^e House? If you know not ye respect due to a Court of Justice, I will teach you, we have power to make you know it.
Dr. F. :	Good my L^{ds}! I ask yr^e Ld^{ps} in all humility to speak but a few words more.
Ld. Ch.:	We have nothing to say to you, hold yr^e peace, Sir; officers, take him away, he is mad.

Undeterred by this abuse, Fairfax insisted that both the presidency and his own fellowship were 'lay affairs' of which

32. Macray, *Register*, iv. 39, 99-102; *DNB*. Fairfax was elected as Ingledew fellow 1659, and served as vice-president 1677. His family pride was shown by his composition *circa* 1660 of a Latin verse panegyric of Sir Thomas Fairfax, who had taken steps to preserve the Bodleian Library at the time of the city's surrender to parliament's forces in 1646.

the commission could have no cognizance and that his cause lay in the courts of Westminster Hall, before he was forcibly 'pull'd away' from the presence of the commissioners.[33]

Aldworth and the others did not follow Fairfax's line. They concentrated their fire instead on Farmer's lack of qualifications and his alleged immorality, on the wholly regular conduct of Hough's election and on their oaths as fellows which had prevented them from obeying the king's mandate. Aldworth's knowledge as a civil lawyer was now advantageous. His able and extensive 'Notes' show his awareness of the stronger and weaker elements in the college's case, and he also asked Hough, who from the outset was regarded as the college's directing mind, to collect detailed evidence from witnesses as to Farmer's past and behaviour.[34] Jeffreys acknowledged Aldworth's legal skills by a characteristic outburst when Aldworth asked for time to consult the college's counsel, Sergeant Edward Byrche (Hough's uncle): this, Jeffreys said, 'was like a man of his coat (Aldworth a civilian) first to do an ill thing, and then to advise with counsel to defend it'.[35] The college's defence made no impression on the commissioners who on 22 June declared Hough's election void and ordered his removal from the presidency. Furthermore, Aldworth was suspended from the vice-presidency and the contumacious Fairfax from his fellowship.

There was now a month's stalemate. By pawning 630 ounces of plate to Daniel Porter, an Oxford goldsmith, the college raised £150 'to supply ye present exigence' (doubtless the extraordinary and heavy legal and other expenses), it being agreed by the president and fellows that within a year either the plate should be redeemed or 'ye same quantity in weight & fashion repurchased'.[36] By deliberate oversight disguised with adroit excuses, the college failed to publish the commission's

33. Magdalen College MS 432, anonymous account, 13 June 1687.

34. *Magdalen and James*, 54, 56-66.

35. *The Diary of Dr Thomas Cartwright, Bishop of Chester*, ed. Joseph Hunter (Camden Society, 1843), 59-60 (6 June 1687).

36. Magdalen College MS, Draft Libri Computi, 19 July 1687, note of sealing of a bill of sale. The accounts for 1687 (Liber Computi 1684-1696) record the large sums of £283:1:10 to meet judicial costs incurred in London and £68:6:6 to cover the costs of fellows' 'equitantibus in Collegii negotiis', presumably in attending the commission in London, securing witnesses etc..

orders of 22 June: these were not fixed to the college gate (by a court officer) until 4 August, so that Hough remained in effective possession of the presidency.

The commissioners tackled Farmer's case on 29 July when he was heard before them in Whitehall. He evidently consulted Dr Charles Hedges, a Magdalen man and a leading civil lawyer who played a considerable part in later proceedings, with, as Hedges recorded, 'earnest importunities & withall telling me y^t he did wave (*sic*) ye presidentship & stood only upon his justification & clearing of his reputation, & shewing me a very specious brief with severall affidavits of his sober life & conversation'. The consultation cannot have given Farmer hope. Hedges had heard that 'particular facts were so evidently made out y^t his case could admit of no manner of defence'.[37] The college's charges, supported by the testimony of twenty-nine carefully-marshalled witnesses, reached back to Farmer's Cambridge days and ranged over his brief career at Oxford. Evidence, much of it perhaps necessarily hearsay, was produced of his quarrelsome behaviour at Magdalen Hall and of his leading William Bambrigge, a gentleman commoner of the Hall, and others into debaucheries in London: in particular there was the shocking charge that he had exposed a naked woman to them. His religious record looked decidedly dubious. After leaving Cambridge he had taught in an unlicensed school at Chippenham in Wiltshire kept by a Protestant nonconformist preacher, his kinsman Benjamin Flower. It appeared from accounts of his conversation that his newly-adopted Catholicism was a pretence in order to get preferment. The under-porter of Magdalen, Robert Gardner, had informed one of the fellows (George Fulham) that Farmer was often incapably drunk in college. Other witnesses testified that with his

37. Magdalen College MS 249, Buckley MSS (papers of Dr, later Sir Charles Hedges), fo. 89v, Hedges' draft defence of his work as king's counsel in the Magdalen case. He was B.A. Magdalen Hall 1670, M.A. Magdalen College 1673, D.C.L. 1675 and was appointed chancellor of the diocese of Rochester 1686. He had defended Compton of London before the commission and also appeared for Cambridge; he had, he writes, 'missed' being counsel for Magdalen by being 'out of town' when the college was cited. His relations with the college remained friendly throughout (see below p. 59, n. 59, for his assistance to Hough). For his interesting role and opinions at important points in the case, see below pp. 56-7, 64-5). He later went on to a successful political career, serving as secretary of state 1700-6.

companions he had behaved improperly and drunkenly in taverns in Abingdon, on one occasion 'much concerned in drink' kissing Martha Mortimer, the landlady of the 'Lobster', 'which he being a stranger she permitted him to do', but then putting his tongue in her mouth: 'such a rudeness, that she immediately went out of his company and would not come nigh him anymore', and on another occasion being involved with others in throwing the town stocks into Mad Hall's Pool. Farmer denied all the charges as unfounded, suborned, malicious or based on hearsay.[38]

It was perhaps hard that the episode in the Cambridge dancing school of some nine years earlier ('such admonitions and acknowledgements are frequent' at Trinity, so he said) should have been raked up and held against him. And it is possible that his quarrels at Magdalen Hall were the result, as he claimed, of its fellows' envy and fears about his gaining 'the tuition and care of many pupils'.[39] He certainly did not deserve Macaulay's denunciation which soared beyond the available evidence:

> This man's life had been a series of shameful acts... He had escaped expulsion [from Cambridge] only by a timely retreat. [At Oxford he] had soon become notorious there for every kind of vice. He generally reeled into his college at night speechless with liquor. He was celebrated for having headed a disgraceful riot at Abingdon. He had been a constant frequenter of noted haunts of libertines. At length he had turned pandar, had exceeded even the ordinary vileness of his vile calling, and had received money from dissolute young gentlemen commoners for services such as it is not good that history should record. This wretch, however, had pretended to turn Papist. His apostasy atoned for all his vices...[40]

John Paget, Macaulay's perceptive contemporary critic, remarked of this passage that 'The impetuous torrent of abuse sweeps the offence out of sight...Lord Macaulay almost leads us

38. *Magdalen and James*, 69-74.
39. Ibid. 72-3.
40. Macaulay, *History*, ii. 248.

to forget how contemptible a person Anthony Farmer really was'.[41] The truth may well be that the twenty-nine year-old Farmer was not so much 'contemptible' as a disappointed and volatile young man, of modest origins and evidently not lacking in ability or intellectual interests, who saw his chance of carving out a career as a Catholic *de convenance* under the new and adventurous regime. Further interesting pieces of information have come to light about him which although they were available to the editors, are not to be found in *Magdalen College and King James II*. He volunteered at the time of Monmouth's rebellion (and may have served under Bagshaw in the college's company). His standing in Magdalen before the presidential election seems to have been perfectly sound. He had been supported in November 1685 by ten of the fellows for a living; and in October 1686 he was given a testimonial signed by Aldworth and eleven others for a fellowship at All Souls in which his sedulous attention to his academic studies and his loyalty in volunteering in 1685 were mentioned.[42] A small but not insignificant token of his good standing in college before the election is his signature in the Inventory Book on 24 May 1686 when borrowing the Frewen tankard; he duly returned it on 9 August 1687 after his official disgrace.[43]

He defended himself with some spirit before the commissioners. There was an affidavit from Bambrigge denying that Farmer had ever enticed him to London or shown him a naked woman: Farmer had always behaved 'as became a sober, modest, & grave Gentleman'. It may be thought that Bambrigge had a strong interest in exculpating himself. As to the testimony of the porter Gardner about Farmer's alleged drunkenness and 'unseasonable' hours, the Catholic fellow Charnock and two demies testified that on being 'desired ingeniously to confess' what he knew about these matters, Gardner 'was surprized att the thing being putt to him and did declare that hee was never askt the question before in his life' —

41. John Paget, *The New Examen* (Haworth Press, 1934), 170-1.

42. Magdalen College MS 249, fo. 83, testimonial 23 Oct. 1686: '...sedulo studiis Operam navasse; et quod ad fidelitatem Spectat, in nupera Rebellione pro Rege ultra Arma Suscepisse.'

43. Magdalen College MS CP2/38, Inventory of all the Colledge Goods, 1659-87, under dates in text.

the implication being that his evidence had been maliciously suborned: in fact, Gardner's recorded reply is cautiously ambiguous and does not clear Farmer.[44] Some of his friends tried to stand by him, but there was altogether too much to explain away. Obadiah Walker and Farmer's other main backers who were in court remained silent: they must have found the experience less than agreeable. Jeffreys listened to the evidence 'very calmly'. His verdict was that the commissioners considered Farmer 'a very bad man'.[45] Farmer's disgrace arose as much from other men's misjudgement of him and from the Catholic interest's shortage of suitable candidates for important offices as from his own failings. With his character destroyed, he passes out of the story and out of the historical record.

The college's disobedience in refusing to elect Farmer was now quietly dropped. The king's need to find another candidate must have been obvious well before the elimination of Farmer. John Dryden was seriously interested in the headship of an Oxford college at this time, and a newsletter of 30 June actually recorded that 'a Mandate is said to be gone down [to] Oxford for Mr. Dryden to go out Doctor of Divinity and also that he will be made President of Magdalen College'. He was the most celebrated (or notorious) of Catholic converts, and statutorily unqualified for the presidency. What the college's reaction might have been to so remarkable a candidate can only be guessed at, for while his claims may have been pressed by his friends and considered by the king and Sunderland, the great poet did not get the nomination. 'The same parts and application which have made me a poet', he wrote sardonically in 1693, 'might have raised me to any honours of the gown which are often given to men of as little learning and less honesty than myself'.[46]

---

44. Magdalen College MS 249, fos. 72, 86, affidavits of Bambrigge (7 July 1687), and of Robert Charnock, Samuel Jenefar and Charles Dormer (25 June 1687); see also ibid. fo. 80, Walker's certificate, 29 June 1687, to the effect that Farmer had never requested any assistance from him in respect of the presidency or any other preferment, to Walker's 'best remembrance'.

45. *Magdalen and James*, 79.

46. See Charles Ward, *The Life of John Dryden* (Chapel Hill, 1961), 233; Roswell G. Ham, 'Dryden and the Colleges', *Modern Language Notes*, xlix (1934), 324-32. Ham suggests that John Dryden Jr's fellowship (below p. 65)

On 14 August, Sunderland sent the king's mandate to the college to admit the bishop of Oxford forthwith as president. Samuel Parker, appointed to Oxford in October 1686, was a candidate of a wholly different stripe to Farmer or Dryden, sharing with them only the fact that he too had never been a fellow of either Magdalen or New College. Now in genuinely poor health, he was a man of powerful and adventurous intellect. Nobody who had read his well-known *Discourse of Ecclesiastical Politie* (1670) could doubt his monarchism, although many might have been alarmed by his extreme views on the necessity of subjecting religion to civil authority, on which vital issue he plainly owed a debt to Hobbes's theory of sovereignty. Even more alarming to orthodox churchmen was his vigorous support for religious toleration. Bishop Burnet described him as 'full of satirical vivacity', but that otherwise he was covetous, ambitious and 'as to religion, rather impious'. Burnet's pen was prejudiced as well as victorious. Parker had been chaplain to Archbishop Sheldon, no mean recommendation. He was encouraged by James's policies of toleration which seemed similar to his own views, and tried without success to get the clergy in Oxford to thank the king for his declaration in favour of liberty of conscience. Historians have said little about him, but the general implications that he was a time-serving crypto-Romanist and an uninteresting man are unjust. There could be much truth as well as proper generosity in Dr Green's view that Parker's writings suggest 'a man of wide learning and of broad tolerance to whom less than justice may have been done'.[47]

To the king's mandate in Parker's favour the current senior fellow, Pudsey, replied that the fellows 'humbly' conceived that they already had a president. Less than a week after this

was perhaps a sop for his father's disappointment, Ward that in allowing his son to take up a fellowship, Dryden was revealing his approval of the king's policies and bringing down more attacks on himself as a turncoat. (I am grateful to Dr David Norbrook for these references.)

47. Green, *Religion at Oxford and Cambridge*, 165; *DNB*, quoting Burnet. Parker took his B.A. at Wadham, moving to Trinity where he exchanged his presbyterianism for warm Anglicanism. His cynical reputation rests largely on the reply he is said to have made to the question 'What was the best body of Divinity?': 'That which would help a man to keep a coach and six horses was certainly the best', quoted in *DNB*; see 'Table Talk...of Hough', 392-3, for other examples of such witticisms.

answer there took place James's visit to Oxford, his furious summons on 4 September to the fellows to elect Parker and their refusal to do so.

On the following day William Penn, the leader of the Quakers who was in Oxford with the king, rode down to Magdalen and into the affair. In view of Penn's closeness to the Court it is difficult not to believe that his intervention at this delicate time was at the suggestion of one of James's advisers, perhaps Parker, with the aim of sounding out the real strength of the fellows' views.[48] It is of course possible that he offered his services on his own initiative: an extraordinary combination of visionary, entrepreneur, scholar, soldier and courtier, he was perfectly capable of such independent action, and his first contact with the fellows was through Charles Goring, a demy of the college. In his general condemnation of Penn's political conduct during the reign, Macaulay claims that Penn intervened as James's agent in order to induce the fellows to obey the king. This is an unfair and untenable view. Penn quickly and clearly pointed out to the king the fellows' difficulty: they could not obey him without breaking their oaths.[49] His mediation appeared particularly sinister because of its coincidence during September with quasi-official intimidation and blandishments. These took the form of rumours that the king was about to issue a writ of *quo warranto* against the college's charter which could lead to the dissolution of the college, together with a list of subtle queries sent anonymously to the fellows on 15 September from the Court at Windsor. These raised various legalistic points and intimated that the fellows, misled by 'hot-headed advisers', were perhaps not acting in the best interests of the college. Would it not be sensible to waive an election and 'admit' Parker, however

---

48. Magdalen College MS 418, fo. 513, Johnston Papers, Sunderland to Parker, 9 Sept. 1687 (copy), committing consideration of the Magdalen case to Parker, Walker and Massey. Sunderland evidently thought that a settlement might be possible; he construed a further address of the fellows (6 Sept.) as meaning that while they could not elect Parker, they would obey him if he were made president by the king: *Magdalen and James*, 92, 94-5.

49. Macaulay, *History*, ii. 255-8; *Magdalen and James*, 88, 93. For Paget's criticism of Macaulay's 'perversions' of the facts and Macaulay's refusal to retract his views of Penn, see Paget, *New Examen*, 169-85, and G. O. Trevelyan, *Life and Letters of Lord Macaulay* (Oxford, 1961 edn.), ii. 188.

suspect as to popery he might be, rather than to 'have all the places of the College refilled by the King's sole authority with Popish Novices and Priests'? Why not make use of 'Mr Penn, or another favourite, [to] prevent the destruction of the best Foundation in Europe'? The fellows held firm against these pressures. They replied on 25 September by re-stating their case as to the statutory requirements and precedents in presidential elections, insisting that headships and fellowships were temporal possessions unimpeachable by summary proceedings and arguing that the commissioners must act according to the laws, 'for *Magna Charta* provides for our Spiritual Liberties as well as our Temporal'.[50]

When Hough, three fellows and Goring met in a three hours' conference with Penn at Windsor on 9 October, Hough was evidently suspicious and dreaded an offer of 'accommodation', not unreasonably when Penn hinted at Hough's perhaps being interested in the bishopric of Oxford in succession to the ailing Parker. Penn, genuinely if naively anxious to open university education to others besides Anglicans, misjudged those he was dealing with, but the worst he can be charged with is that he was a well-intentioned and unsuccessful peacemaker. He protested his concern for the college's welfare, emphasised his 'many efforts' to reconcile the fellows to the king, and suggested implausibly that Jeffreys rather than Sunderland (Penn's old Christ Church crony) was to blame for the quarrel. This line of talk was too much for Hough:

> Mr Penn, in this I will be plain with you. We have our Statutes and Oaths to justify us in all we have done hitherto; but setting this aside, we have a Religion to defend, and I suppose that you yourself would think us Knaves if we should tamely give it up. The Papists have already got Christ-Church and University College: the present struggle is for Magdalen, and they threaten that in a short time they will have the rest.

This plain speaking must have jolted Penn who vehemently assured Hough that if the Papists 'proceed so far', they would lose his and others' support; but he then added, as Hough

50. *Magdalen and James*, 96-101.

thought 'either off his guard, or [having] a mind to droll upon us':

> I suppose two or three Colleges will content the papists: Christ Church is a noble structure, University College is a pleasant place, and Magdalen College is a comely building. The walks are pleasant and it is conveniently situated just at the entrance of the Town &c.

Hough's reply was brisk and to the point. When the Papists had Magdalen, 'they would take the rest, as they and the present possessors could never agree'. He did not tell Penn what he added to his correspondent:

> In short, I see that it is resolved that the papists must have our College, and I think all that we have to do is, to let the world see that they *take* it from us, and that we do not *give* it up.[51]

With the failure of Penn's good offices, the king's commissioners set about 'taking' the college. Hough and the fellows were cited to undergo their visitation on 21 October. Thomas Cartwright, bishop of Chester, the closest of the bishops to James and fully sharing his notions of royal power, was appointed to lead the visitation. He was a grandson of Thomas Cartwright, the celebrated Elizabethan puritan, and like Parker at Wadham he had been influenced by puritan teachings during his undergraduate career at Queen's. His diary reveals an energetic, convivial, naively ambitious man who made up in self-important dogmatism for what he lacked in personal and intellectual weight. As dean of Ripon he had supported James stoutly before and during the Exclusion crisis of 1679-81, and obtained his reward with the important see of Chester in October 1686. Although this appointment had scandalised many churchmen, there is no suggestion that he was ever inclined to Romanism or indeed that he was anything more than a high-flying, literally-minded monarchist. In London he was certainly on close terms with the vicar-apostolic John Leyburn, bishop of Adremetum, with Father Edward Petre, James's Jesuit confidant who became a privy councillor

---

51. Hough to a cousin, 9 Oct. [1687], *Magdalen and James*, 104-6.

in November 1687, and with the judges Sir Richard Allibone and Sir Robert Wright; his relations with Jeffreys seem to have been poor. On his appointment to head the visitation of Magdalen, he was delighted to receive the congratulations of his friends 'for having got the King's favour, after which all other things would be added to me', by which he meant the vacant archbishopric of York.[52]

His colleagues were the two judges Sir Robert Wright and Sir Thomas Jenner. Wright, a protegé of Jeffreys, had served as a judge on the Bloody Assizes; his record on the bench showed his support for all the king's policies, and in April 1687 he replaced Herbert as lord chief justice of King's Bench. Jenner was a second choice of James and his closest advisers. They had first asked Charles Hedges who fortunately left an account (hitherto unpublished) of his interview on 14 October in William Chiffin's chambers in Whitehall with the king, Jeffreys and Sunderland while Cartwright and Wright waited in an outer room. After Jeffreys had warmly recommended Hedges to James (and Sunderland had added: 'very fit...& I take it, expert in his P[ro] fession'), Hedges was told by Jeffreys that the business in hand was to visit Magdalen in order to turn out Hough and admit the bishop of Oxford. James cut in: 'And to turn out yᵉ others. I have been affronted & abus'd more than ever K[ing] was, & I would have my honour vindicated'. Hedges begged not to be sent as a commissioner: it would damage his practice in which he said far too modestly that he was 'but a beginner', and he had a wife and family to provide for. Moreover, although he agreed that the college's behaviour constituted 'a great contempt' of the king's sovereignty, he gave his opinion that the college was 'enabled by law to do' what it had done and that Hough's election could not be made void. This reply surprised and displeased his hearers, Sunderland remarking that 'What we did [in ordering Hough's removal from the presidency on 22 June] was upon yʳ opin[ion]. You know we advised with you before we gave sentence, & this is very strange'. Hedges replied that his advice had related to the king's dispensing power, not to the punishment of the college; Sunderland insisted that 'we advised upon' both the power and the punishment. James, by

52. Cartwright, *Diary*, 85 (14 Oct. 1687).

now evidently bewildered, remarked that 'Here is something more in this business than I understand'. But although he went on to tell Hedges that 'I allways have occasion for a civilian in my business, & have been no ill master to those [lawyers] I have employed', he ended the interview by saying generously: 'I will not press you, I'll assure y^{e}'.[53] Hedges no doubt felt much relieved. But with his opinions he must have appeared to James and his advisers as a less than reliable choice, and his name was struck out of the commission. Jenner, formerly recorder of London and recently promoted to the bench as a baron of the Exchequer, went as commissioner in his place. Hedges served instead as counsel for the king in the case.

Cartwright took his instructions directly from the king, Jeffreys and Sunderland, receiving papers from and discussing the business also with Father Petre.[54] The commissioners entered Oxford on 20 October with an escort of three troops of horse of Lord Peterborough's regiment which was quartered in the city, and took up their lodgings in Mr Brooks's house 'over against' the Blue Boar. Next day they went down to Magdalen, and after finding that no preparations had been made for conducting their business in the chapel, began proceedings in the hall in the presence of 'a great crowd' which pressed almost to the elbows of the commissioners who sat on the further side of the high table, with Cartwright flanked by his colleagues. Cartwright complained not unreasonably of the behaviour of a doctor of divinity: 'little respect could be expected from ye younger part', he said, 'when a Dr...was so rude as to stand on ye table'.[55] When order was obtained with the help of the proctors, Cartwright read a long address to the fellows lasting nearly half an hour and containing the purest milk of the doctrine of divine right. The king was God's minister to whom absolute and unconditional loyalty was owed: he was 'the Father of our country,...the Centre of the Kingdom'; the college like all other corporations was 'the Creature of the Crown; and how then

---

53. Magdalen College MS 249, fos. 91-2, Hedges' notes, 14 Oct. 1687; and fo. 94, notes, 9 Oct. 1687, for his pleas to Jeffreys as to his practice and family.

54. Cartwright, *Diary*, 83-4, 86 (13, 14, 18 Oct. 1687). It does not appear what Petre's 'papers' contained. This is one of the few known instances of Petre's intervention in political matters.

55. Magdalen College MS 249, fos. 8-9v, Hedges' notes.

1. PETER MEWS, BISHOP OF WINCHESTER

John Hough D.D.
Bishop of Worcester

2. PRESIDENT HOUGH

3. PRESIDENT GIFFARD

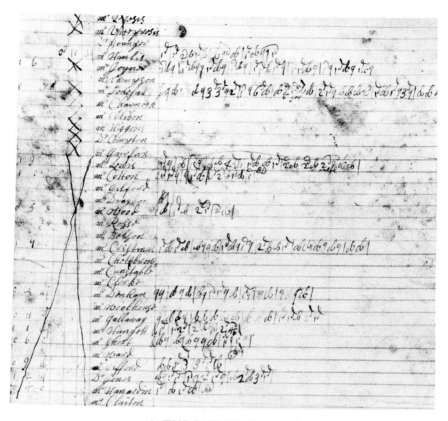

4. THE BUTTERY BOOK
week beginning 20 October 1688, with Bishop Mews' crosses
against the intruded President and Fellows

durst you make your Statutes spurn against their Maker?'
'Profaneness', he told them, was a greater danger to the nation
than popery. His address showed his awareness of the national
importance of the matter: he warned the fellows that the eyes of
the world were upon them, and 'they ought to take care, how
their practices might influence their deluded admirers'. And he
exhorted them solemnly 'in the Bowels of Christ' to 'a more
entire submission and obedience'.[56]

It was a cardinal point in the college's case that the king
could not order a visitation where there was a local Visitor.
Hough, described as 'modest, calm and yet assured', told the
commissioners that he and the greater part of the fellows
submitted to the visitation 'so far as it is consistent with the
Laws of the Land, and the Statutes of the College, and no
further' — or in other words that they did not submit to it. In
answer to the chief justice he refused to agree that the king
could dispense with or alter the college's statutes or his own
obligation to obey them. To Cartwright, who claimed that the
Crown had 'for the most part' recommended persons for the
presidency, he said that he was the twentieth president, and
only four of that number had been so recommended, 'whereof
three were everyway qualified'. He protested that by the
commission's decree of 22 June he was to be deprived of his
freehold without being either summoned or heard.[57]

Next day, the 22nd, in the present common room to which
the commissioners had adjourned (the hall was found too
public), Hough was seen in private and advised to yield quietly.
Protesting his loyalty to the king but again insisting on his
possession of his freehold 'according to the Laws of England,
and the Statutes of the College', he refused to resign or to give
up the keys of his office and the Lodgings.[58] In the presence of
the fellows he was then formally expelled, and his name was
struck out of the Buttery Book. At two o'clock that day the
fellows were asked if they would now admit the bishop of
Oxford as president. Only Charnock and Thompson agreed to
do so; Pudsey and Thomas Smith gave equivocal answers, and

56. *Magdalen and James*, 114-7. Almont recorded Cartwright's warning and
words about public opinion: Magdalen College MS 908/26, 19 Oct. 1687.
57. *Magdalen and James*, 120-1, 124.
58. Ibid. 127-9.

the rest refused. At this point, Hough entered the common room followed by a crowd of 'Strangers & young Scholars' and asked if he might say a few words. With a proper sense of theatre, the commissioners gave him leave to do so and 'put off their hats'. Hough then declared:

> My Lords,...I do hereby Protest against all your Proceedings, and against all that you have done, or hereafter shall do, in prejudice of me and my Right, as illegal, unjust and null, and therefore I appeal to my Sovereign Lord the King in his Courts of Justice.[59]

The crowd, crammed into a relatively small room, greeted this speech with 'a great hume & acclamation'.[60] Despite Hough's doubtless genuine denial that he had had anything to do with the crowd's behaviour, the incensed chief justice announced that he would defend the king's authority 'while he had blood in his body'; and claiming that Hough had broken the king's peace 'by his popular Protest', he bound him over in his own bond of £1000 and two others of £500 each to appear before him in King's Bench in due course.[61]

The fellows now faced the problem of their attitude to the imminent mandate for Parker's admission as president. Fairfax was in a unique position: already suspended, he had briskly defended his refusal to elect Farmer whom he described as 'such a virtuoso', and announced his intention to seek relief in the chief justice's own court, his fellowship being, like Hough's office, a freehold. When Jenner reminded him that legal action 'requir's a purse', Fairfax, evidently an experienced litigant, replied: 'I did not say I was poor'.[62]

Parker lay ill and *hors de combat* at Cuddesdon when the

---

59. Ibid. 136. Hough was denied a copy of his various statements to the commissioners, but Hedges privately gave him one from his own notes, and told him that he would testify to the truth of it at any time; Hough 'should have nothing put upon him y^t he did not say': Magdalen College MS 249, fos. 89v-90.

60. Magdalen College MS 249, fo. 32, Hedges' notes. A 'hum' in the seventeenth century could signify popular approval or disapproval. On this occasion it plainly signified strong support of Hough's statement.

61 *Magdalen and James*, 137.

62. Magdalen College MS 908/26, Almont's account: Fairfax added that he had been 'above 4 years' in all the courts of Westminster Hall, '& found excellent justice, & will see how it is now'; *Magdalen and James*, 129-31.

mandate for his admission as president reached the commissioners on the 25th. That morning, in their presence and in Charnock's alone of the fellows, he was admitted and installed in the chapel by proxy, his chaplain William Wickens taking all the required oaths on his behalf. A comedy was then played out to give Mr Wickens possession of the Lodgings as the new president's proxy. According to the fellows, the only people who had the keys were Hough's servants, none of whom appeared; the fellows said that they themselves had no key; and the tipstaff told Cartwright that the first blacksmith fetched in order to break into the Lodgings had run as fast as he could out of the back gate as soon as the tipstaff's back was turned. A second smith was then sent for, who forced the door, and the keys were found safely inside.

The commissioners returned to the common room, and at once put to the fellows the grave question as to whether they would obey the new president. Thomas Smith alone gave in an entire submission. The rest (twenty-five) asked for time to consider, and met in the hall. There is no record of their discussions, but when they were called into the common room later that afternoon they produced an answer signed by them all in which they submitted to Parker on the formula, devised by themselves, 'so far as is lawful and agreeable to the Statutes'. The demies, chaplains, choristers and clerks submitted in identical terms. The fellows wanted to add that their submission was in no way prejudicial to Hough's future right and title, but were assured by the learned judges that this was superfluous. Fairfax, still denying the commission's authority and refusing to submit on any terms, was deprived of his fellowship and expelled with a fortnight's grace. Robert Gardner, the porter whose evidence had been so helpful in discrediting Farmer, likewise refused to submit and was deprived of his post with three days' notice.[63]

The commissioners, who had also been ordered to inquire whether the college had misapplied its revenues or broken the statutes in other ways, were able almost at once to certify that they were satisfied in these respects, and they reported to Sunderland on the 25th that the college was settled and 'in good

63. *Magdalen and James*, 147-58.

temper'. Most of the fellows had indeed followed the path of 'passive obedience', and it was hardly fair that great dissatisfaction should now have been expressed in tory Oxford at their submission. Walker and the Catholics naturally taunted the fellows with their lack of courage, but there were also scornful references by ordinary citizens to 'your Magdalen College conscience'.[64] A sympathetic contemporary, Thomas Tramallier of Jesus, 'was surpris'd, I must confess, to see it come to this; but I dare not judge them... they have thereby shew'd the king a way to putt into every place; not to say, That in it's consequence it affects every man's Property in England'.[65] This was a shrewd assessment. The Magdalen conscience was quickly to be put to even more severe trial.

On the 27th Sunderland sent by express from Whitehall further instructions from the king to the commissioners. These arrived next day. The fellows were to be required on pain of expulsion to address the king asking James's pardon 'for their late offences and obstinacy' and, far more important, acknowledging the commission's jurisdiction and the legality of its proceedings. Hough and Fairfax were to be further punished by being incapacitated from all future preferment, and two Roman Catholics were to be appointed to fellowships.[66] These orders have often been seen as egregious examples of James's personal vindictiveness. This charge can only properly be linked to the punishment of Hough and Fairfax. The other orders were a logical part of James's strategy of establishing Catholics in positions within the universities and, more broadly, of clamping royal authority on all institutions. The Magdalen fellows had submitted on their own terms to the new president but the great majority had not explicitly acknowledged the commission's legality and the king's powers, while Hough and Fairfax had publicly denied both. James and Sunderland needed such an acknowledgement from the college as a clear precedent to enable them to continue their policies first in Magdalen and then elsewhere.

The fellows must have been shaken by reactions in Oxford to

64. Smith's Diary, 28 Oct. 1687, ibid. 173.
65. T. Tramallier to Lord Hatton, 27 Oct. 1687, ibid. 167.
66. Ibid. 169.

their submission, but their discussions were also influenced by the menacing nature of James's new and unexpected demands. They had gone far to meet his wishes, and would go no further. They were now to show a particularly creditable kind of courage, for the promises of support from high quarters ('great men') in London had not yet reached them. Prompted by Thomas Bayley, one of the seniors, the fellows refused to acknowledge any error or to ask for pardon: in electing Hough they had observed their statutes, nor would they acknowledge the commission's jurisdiction. Most added that their submission to Parker did not mean that they would obey him as president but merely that they did not oppose the kingly authority which had put him in. One junior fellow, George Fulham, hotly denied the legality of Parker's admission and was suspended from his fellowship for what Cartwright called his 'contempt and opprobrious language'. Another junior fellow, Henry Holden, now saw that 'without God's interposing Providence...the ruin of Magdalen College is to be expected'.[67] This was also clear to one of the commissioners. Jenner was politically much the least weighty of them. Overawed, as he wrote in his diary, by the 'great and most difficult affairs' of state in which he had become involved and uncomfortably aware of the invidiousness of his duty, he had already had several sharp disagreements with the overbearing Cartwright about the further proceedings against the college after Hough's expulsion, and he was dismayed by the requirements in Sunderland's express of the 27th.[68] It must have been some temporary relief to him when matters were adjourned until 16 November.

When the commissioners returned to Magdalen, escorted again by cavalry, President Parker had moved into the Lodgings. The fellows' petition, a complete submission and acknowledgement of the commissioners' authority, had been drafted for them. Any man refusing to sign it would be expelled. In the common room on the morning of the 16th, Cartwright once again delivered a long homily to the fellows: 'No Society of men in this or the other University ever had so many

67. Ibid. 169-72, 175-7.
68. Ibid. 143, 145, 175-6, 211 n.l.

malcontents and mutineers', he informed them, and he referred not only to their recent 'petulant humour and contumacious behaviour', but to their 'continual' quarrels with presidents, Visitors and among themselves ever since 1660; he expatiated on the king's piety, goodness and mercy.[69] Aldworth, the suspended vice-president, now returned to give his colleagues a lead. He had carefully worked out his position, as his draft notes and consultation with his brother, also a lawyer, testify. Before the commissioners he took his stand on the college's statutes confirmed by monarchs before and since the Reformation. To admit 'a Stranger & a Foreigner' would be to give up 'ye rights of ye Coll. & of all o[u]r Successors'.[70] When Cartwright claimed that the statutes were overruled by the king's authority, Aldworth replied that 'Our Statutes...are agreeable to the King's Laws both Ecclesiastical and Civil, and so long as we live up to them, we obey the King'.[71] For his part he could not submit to Parker as president. Thomas Smith, Charnock and Thompson had already submitted, but all the rest followed Aldworth in refusing to sign the submission. Twenty-five fellows were accordingly deprived and expelled, and their names were struck out of the Buttery Book.[72] They registered a formal protest against the commissioners' proceedings and their intention to use all legal means of redress. It must have been some comfort to them that the demies made it clear through Thomas Holt, the senior demy, that they would not obey the president. The fellows may also have known that Gilbert Ironside, the vice-chancellor and warden of Wadham,

69. Ibid. 185-90.

70. Ibid. 179-81; Magdalen College MS 908/26, [16 Nov. 1687], Almont's account.

71. *Magdalen and James*, 206.

72. The eight fellows not present and not then deprived produced valid certificates for their absence. Maynard, for example, was chaplain to Lord Digby, Francis Smith was travelling abroad with Lord Brooke. Of these, Charles Hawles alone later submitted to President Parker. There were two special cases. Younger was excused appearing because of his attendance as chaplain on Princess Anne (it would have created a serious family problem for James if one so close to his daughter had been deprived), and he was thus in no need of subsequent restoration. The elderly William Hooper was regarded as mentally 'distracted' and took no part in college proceedings: he received a regular annual allowance of £26. For his charity and other virtues, including his planting of elms and gardening, see Bloxam, *Register*, v. 150-2. One fellowship was vacant through Thomas Ludford's death in the preceding month.

had declined an invitation to dine with the commissioners on the day of the fellows' expulsion with the explanation that 'he did not like with Colonel Kirk to dine under the gallows'.[73]

Using the royal mandate, the commissioners had already admitted two Catholics as fellows: William Joyner, a fellow over forty years earlier who lost his fellowship by turning Catholic, and Job Allibone, a brother of Sir Richard the judge; two demies (one, Samuel Jenefar, a crony of Farmer), described as 'so-called Protestants', were also made fellows at this time. Joyner and Allibone were dispensed by the king from the oaths of allegiance and supremacy. As with the Declaration of Indulgence which was to lead to the trial of the Seven Bishops in June 1688, so with the case of the fellows of Magdalen the heart of the matter was whether the king's authority could override existing legislation. If it could, then all offices in church and state, in a real sense all property, were at his disposal: no man could plead freehold rights against his authority. In London and elsewhere men talked of James's arbitrary government. He was indeed fully launched on his 'revolutionary attack on the existing political order'.[74]

As if to underline this, Hough and the expelled fellows were declared on 12 December by the commission in Whitehall to be incapacitated for all ecclesiastical appointments. But this decision was reached by the commission only after several discussions and by a majority of one, with Herbert and Jenner among those voting against the measure, Sunderland, Jeffreys, Cartwright and Wright in favour. At a conference in Chiffin's chambers six days earlier, Hedges had given an emphatic legal opinion against further proceedings to incapacitate the fellows: as the king summarised Hedges' view, 'they cannot be farther punished, because they have been punished allready'. It was Sunderland who suggested, as he had earlier, that the expulsion of the fellows was carried out by the commissioners 'only as visitors' and not as ecclesiastical commissioners, 'so y^t they may yet be punish'd by eccles[iastical] censure'. To this Hedges replied that in his view their offence was not ecclesiastical, 'but if it were... y^r Lordships have proceeded in both capacities'

73. *Magdalen and James*, 217.
74. Miller, *Popery and Politics*, 222.

already.[75] The majority in the commission who voted for further punishment did so against the advice of the king's counsel in the case. A less determined, more realistic ruler than James would have paid close attention to these signs of division and disquiet among his most senior officials.

In Magdalen the president and the temporarily shrunken body of fellows (Smith left at once for London) faced the persistent and annoying hostility of the demies who refused to recognise the authority of Parker, Charnock the vice-president or Charles Hawles the dean. They would not 'cap' the fellows, ran their own disputations and other exercises, and read prayers in the chapel. There were disorders and acts of defiance in Hall. They courted expulsion which came to fourteen of them on 17 January and to three more on the 31st. On 31 December the king ordered the president to admit twelve new fellows, all Catholics, including the learned Jesuit Dr Thomas Fairfax, several other priests (among them George Plowden of the ancient family of Plowden Hall in Shropshire), and John Dryden, the poet's second son now aged about twenty who had been a pupil of Obadiah Walker.[76] By the end of March nine more Catholic fellows had been admitted. Parker seems by now to have become dismayed by what he was being ordered to do, and according to a servant's report the command to admit this last batch brought on 'a convulsive fit' from which he never recovered. He died on 21 March at the age of forty-eight. On his death-bed he took the sacrament, telling the Catholic priests that 'he neither was, nor would be of their Communion' and freely declaring to the fellows his 'sincere adherence to the principles of the Church of England'.[77] On 24 March his coffin with six heads of houses holding up the pall was 'carried round the cloister by torchlight, the choristers singing before', and he was buried on the south side of the ante-chapel where Samuel Jenefar 'made a speech...to [the bishop's] great commendation', in the course of which he attacked Andrew Marvell with whom Parker had often crossed swords over issues of political

75. *Magdalen and James*, 222-3; Magdalen College MS 249, fos. 98, 99v-101, Hedges' opinion, 8 Dec., and accounts of conferences 6, 8, Dec. 1687.

76. *Magdalen and James*, 225-30. The king also appointed all the college officers.

77. Ibid. 240-1.

theory.[78] It is likely that Parker was in the end as disillusioned by the practical workings of James's policies of toleration as the king was displeased by the heretical manner of Parker's death.[79]

For the presidency, James nominated Bonaventure Giffard, bishop-elect of Madaura *in partibus* and vicar-apostolic of the midland district, a member of an ancient and notable Staffordshire family whose father had died for the royalist cause early in the Civil War. He was educated at the English college at Douai, received his D.D. from the Sorbonne in 1678 and was appointed one of James's chaplains soon after the king's accession.[80] There was of course no election for Charnock to conduct as vice-president, nor was the redoubtable Visitor troubled by having to admit the new president. Giffard was given extraordinary powers in June to fill fellowships and demyships without the consent or approval of the fellows, and was wholly exempted from the Visitor's authority. In August he used his powers to expel Thomas Smith and six other Anglican fellows not previously expelled. (Younger was left undisturbed; Hawles had submitted: see n. 72.)

For six months the college operated as a Catholic seminary, its pupils coming from the school set up in the Savoy by the king and run by the Jesuit Mr Poulton. Church of England services of a kind had continued after the main expulsion of the fellows, prayers being read by a demy who was an M.A.; after their expulsion, the presence of Parker in the Lodgings prevented mass being said in the chapel. After his death, Thomas Smith's wish to go down to Magdalen and hold Anglican services was blocked by legal advice, and the chapel was turned over to Roman rites on the orders of Charnock as vice-president. Magdalen quickly became the principal focus of Catholic observance in Oxford, although this was not without its difficulties for those conducting the services. According to Wood, 'Many crowded in for noveltie sake to grin and sneare';

78. Wood, *Life and Times*, iii. 261-2 (24 March 1688).

79. *Magdalen and James*, 241, prints hostile and eulogistic epitaphs. There is no memorial to him in the chapel. James said that Parker died 'without any religion' and that many of the bishops were well known to be presbyterians: ibid. 243.

80. He was b.1642, elder son of Andrew Giffard (Gifford) of Chillingworth, Staffs. His younger brother Andrew was a fellow under his presidency. For President Giffard, see further below, esp. pp. 95-103.

M.A.s of other colleges came to fill up the fellows' stalls, while 'many townsmen and women' also attended 'to keep out... the papists'.[81] The university in the person of Warden Ironside acted with formal correctness in accepting the Catholic heads, including Giffard, as members of the hebdomadal board, and Ironside himself dined in Magdalen. But he refused to attend the St Mark's Day sermon on 25 April in the college for which Charnock selected Thomas Fairfax as preacher, telling Charnock that 'Wee shall not then be there to heare e[u]logies on the Virgin Mary'; he appointed his own preacher and attended his rival sermon in St Mary's.[82]

The Catholic fellows endured insulting behaviour to them in the streets and in their own groves and water-walks from 'waggish quarrelsome scholars' and townspeople, and they were forced to order the main entrances to the college to be kept shut — evidence, however deplorable, of the deep-seated popular hatred of Catholicism. Wood also recorded that for 'want of choristers and clerks', there was no May Morning singing from the Tower in 1688 for the first time since the restoration of Charles II.[83] More seriously, indeed ominously for the king's regime, it was noticed that only Magdalen and Christ Church celebrated the birth of the Prince of Wales on 10 June. The position of Giffard and his colleagues cannot have been a comfortable one, although they kept up a brave show. Their gaudy in the hall on 1 July, presided over by the president in his long purple cassock and attended by Catholic army officers, was evidently a splendid if somewhat military affair with trumpets and kettle drums marking the entry of the president, fellows and their guests and each health as it was drunk during the dinner.[84] Time was not given to the college to become what the king and his advisers hoped, 'a place where the true doctrine should be publickly taught, and thence spread consecutively to the other parts of the realm'. Thomas Fairfax was clearly setting about the good work when he engaged in a dispute with John Meddens, B.A., of Wadham, on the doctrine

81. Wood, *Life and Times*, iii. 253-4, 264 (11 Jan., 22 April 1688).
82. Ibid. iii. 265 (23 April 1688).
83. Ibid. iii. 257, 266 (25 Feb., 1 May 1688).
84. Ibid. iii. 271 (1 July 1688).

of purgatory; their recorded dialogue could be read in Hall's coffee house.[85]

What, in the meantime, of the expelled and incapacitated fellows? Macaulay depicts their plight in pathetic terms. James encompassed 'the utter ruin of his victims'. It was not enough to expel them and to strip them of their revenues: '...every walk of life towards which men of their habits could look for a subsistence [was] closed against them with malignant care'. They were reduced to 'the precarious and degrading resource of alms'.[86] The truth is less dramatic and more significant. The Anglican establishment rallied to its own. Subscriptions were set up to which Princess Mary contributed the handsome sum of £200, and the magnates most involved in the university's affairs, Lords Nottingham, Weymouth and Abingdon, were stirred into generosity by Sir Thomas Clarges, the long-serving burgess for the university.[87] Several bishops quietly paid no attention to the ban on the fellows' preferment; eight fellows were taken on as chaplains in the households of various noblemen, and the physician Dr John Smith was allowed £50 per annum by a consortium of supporters. With proper gratitude towards those who had stood by him, Hough busied himself in London with mobilising his connections with wealthy sympathisers; he was so active that he earned the king's displeasure and was forced to leave London for Worcester. Before leaving, he had a stroke of good fortune in King's Bench where he appeared on 5 December on the chief justice's previous order. Wright was not in court, and the sitting judges were Allibone and Sir Richard Holloway. Sergeant Byrche, Hough's counsel, testified that the attorney-general had assured him that he had nothing against Hough's being discharged from the bonds which he and his security had given to keep the peace, and that the chief justice himself had agreed to discharge Hough. Holloway confirmed this testimony as to the chief justice's view: Allibone then duly discharged Hough and his security; but when Wright arrived in court and heard the result, he 'seemed to be in a passion at this and said that the last

85. *Magdalen and James*, 242; Wood, *Life and Times*, iii. 267 (1 June 1688).
86. Macaulay, *History*, ii. 264.
87. Bennett, 'Loyalist Oxford', 19.

night his Majesty had given him order that Dr Huff (*sic*) should not be discharged'. Holloway, when taxed by Allibone with being responsible, was in 'great confusion': still, as the record goes on, 'the business was done', and Hough was a free man.[88]

There is no evidence that any of the expelled fellows suffered seriously in the eleven months of their expulsion. They could not have known of course that this would last so short a time, and they must have felt considerable private anxiety along with their concern for the public issues raised by their case. Thomas Smith probably suffered most. He was known for a time not as 'Dr Tograi' but as 'Dr Roguery', and in London he had to endure vigorous condemnation both of the king's proceedings and his own actions: it was said quite falsely that he was either a papist or after preferment. His eventual expulsion by President Giffard may have restored his credit in some quarters. He was an independent-minded, perhaps somewhat cross-grained person, much more experienced in worldly matters and far better known outside Oxford than nearly all his colleagues. He probably thought that the king would win; he certainly believed that the king's supremacy meant what it said, and that James must be obeyed. His conduct, as he claimed, was consistent with a more extreme interpretation of 'passive obedience' than most of his colleagues would accept, and it is to his credit that his conduct after the Revolution was of a piece with what it had been before it. He merited President Routh's description of him as 'that signal martyr to conscience, who was fated to be a loser, whatever side was uppermost'.[89]

Time and fortune now began to run out for the king. The acquittal of the Seven Bishops was a disaster for him. News of the sufferings of the Huguenots in France increased the fears of English protestants, dissenters as well as Anglicans, about James's policies: it was not only the church of England or the fellows of Magdalen who could be anxious for their religion and property. By the summer of 1688 the government's control of local authorities was crumbling, and a steady, quiet withdrawal of obedience to the Crown was taking place. The stage was set

88. *Calendar of State Papers, Domestic Series, James II*, vol. iii (1687-9), (London, 1972), 109-10.
89. Bloxam, *Register*, iii. 196.

for William of Orange's descent. The bishops including Mews of Winchester pressed James to moderate and even reverse his policies, and one of their first moves on 3 October was to advise him to restore the president and fellows of Magdalen; two days later the ecclesiastical commission was dissolved, and on the 11th Sunderland sent the king's instructions to Mews to restore Hough and his colleagues.[90]

Mews set about his mission willingly but somewhat slowly until he was spurred on by the archbishop of Canterbury and others. On the 20th he entered Oxford with *éclat* and an escort of 300 persons on horseback, 'most of them Scholars, and six or seven coaches, full of Noblemen and Doctors'.[91] But late that night he was summoned to Whitehall in order to witness depositions of the legitimacy of the Prince of Wales on the 22nd. By commanding the presence of Mews and other members of the council, James did not intend to interrupt or countermand the restoration of the college; but it is a significant indication of the general distrust felt for him that it was widely believed at the time (and later stated as a fact by Bishop Burnet) that the delay was connected with news of the storms encountered by William's invasion fleet.[92] The delay was wholly accidental on James's part; it was the result of Mews's decision to obey an urgent summons to Whitehall instead of proceeding, to the strongly-expressed disappointment of the fellows, with his business in Oxford. James was angry when he learnt on the 22nd that the college had not been restored and sent Mews down to Oxford to do it forthwith.

On Thursday 25 October the bishop in his episcopal habit entered the college between 9 and 10 in the morning, and was received by Hough and a large number of the expelled fellows and demies. In chapel, Thomas Bayley made a congratulatory speech in Latin after which Mews performed divine service and then read out the king's order to him to 'settle the College legally and statutably'. He and the assembled company next proceeded to the hall where Mews called for the Buttery Book

90. Leyburn, the vicar-apostolic in London, was also strongly in favour of restoring the college: *Magdalen and James*, 252-3, 253, n.1.

91. Ibid. 254, 256.

92. See ibid. 257-9, esp. Routh's note to Burnet's *History of the Reign of James II.*

and struck out the names of all the Catholic fellows, using single crosses to deal with Giffard and the eight most senior of his colleagues, avoiding the names of the Anglicans Hawles and Thompson who had submitted and of Younger who had never been troubled in any way, and then inscribing one huge cross to deal with twenty-one of the rest. (Plate 4) He ordered the names of all the former fellows to be reinscribed in the Book, and declared Dr Hough to be president: he, the thirty-three reinstated fellows, twenty-four demies, four chaplains, the schoolmaster, the steward, the usher, the organist, eight clerks, sixteen choristers and the servants (including the porter Robert Gardner) were 'the true, legal and statutable Members of the Foundation, and none others'. To great applause Mews recommended the virtues of loyalty and unity to the college, and the president replied 'in a short and pithy speech'.[93]

There is no record of what Hough said, but perhaps he remembered his remarkable conversation exactly a year earlier with the countess of Ossory, the daughter-in-law of his old patron Ormonde. He dined with her shortly after his expulsion:

> ...taking a glass of Moselle wine and moving it under her nose for the flavour (for she never drank any), 'Come Doctor', says she, 'my service to you; be of good courage, 'tis but twelve months to this day twelve-month'. 'Tis certainly so, madam', replied the Doctor, 'but what then?' 'I say no more', says she, 'but remember well what I say; 'tis but twelve months to this day twelve-month'.

Her advice that Hough should remember the exact length of a year turned out to be uncannily good, although it may have reflected her political hopes and those of her son James, duke of Ormonde, as much as second sight.[94]

---

93. Ibid. 260-5.

94. For the anecdote, recorded by Carte after visiting Hough in 1735, see 'Table Talk...of Hough', 413; *Magdalen and James*, 158 (a slightly different version). The countess was Emilia, eldest daughter of the Lord of Beverwaert and a kinswoman of William of Orange with whom her late husband saw much service. Their son James who succeeded his grandfather in July 1688 was a discreet but active supporter of William's interests before the Revolution. After his grandfather's death, he was immediately elected chancellor of Oxford by Convocation before the king was able to send down his mandate in favour of Jeffreys: *DNB* (Butler, Thomas, earl of Ossory; Butler, James, 2nd duke of Ormonde); Bennett, 'Loyalist Oxford', 19.

Later on the day of the restoration, the president provided 'a very gallant dinner' in the Lodgings for the Visitor, the vice-chancellor, some heads of houses and canons of Christ Church (who may have felt that the invitation contained more than mere *politesse*), while the fellows and demies had their gaudy in the hall with music provided at a cost of £2. That night there was a large bonfire in the quadrangle, and according to Wood, 'a great deal of drink' (he thought nine barrels, but he was not sure) '[was] given to the mobile'. The bells, led by Magdalen's, rang throughout the city, and bonfires were lit at Christ Church, Merton and near Trinity, in Eastgate, and no less than twelve in the parish of St Peter's where the college had a number of tenants.[95]

'Thus', as a contemporary put it, 'by the Providence of God, and upon a revolution of affairs, that honest and stout Society...was restaur'd'.[96] The king's concessions in restoring Magdalen, dissolving the ecclesiastical commission and regranting their former charters to the municipal corporations did more serious damage to his regime than he had inflicted on it by his authoritarianism; James's reign and policies proved the wisdom of Lord Salisbury's advice in 1610 to the first Stuart king: 'when a king extendeth his uttermost authority, he loseth his power'.[97] In exile, James was aware that 'this famous dispute' with Magdalen had raised 'so many enemies' for him, but he insisted that he was merely exercising his lawful authority as interpreted by the judges and the civil lawyers, that certain 'violent and factious' fellows among whom he numbered Aldworth, Henry Fairfax, and Pudsey had set out to disobey him, and that by refusing to submit to President Parker they and their colleagues had effectively resigned their fellowships. He did not intend, he said, 'to dispossess the Church of England' of Magdalen: its fellows had formed a confederacy 'only to draw an odium upon their Prince'.[98] This latter charge, a characteristic Jamesian conspiracy theory

95. Macray, *Register*, iv. 43; Wood, *Life and Times*, iii. 533 (25 Oct. 1688).

96. Tramallier to Lord Hatton, Oct.-Nov. 1688, *Magdalen and James*, 256.

97. *Proceedings in Parliament, 1610*, ed. Elizabeth Read Foster (New Haven, 1966), i. 70. (I owe this reference to the kindness of Professor the Earl Russell.)

98. *The Life of James the Second...*(1816), quoted in *Magdalen and James*, 268-70.

which transferred all the blame for his misfortunes to others, was baseless: the fellows' resistance was a final defensive reaction to the king's threats to their religion and their property. James achieved what seemed the least likely outcome in 1685 when tory and Anglican support for the monarchy was so powerful: he virtually destroyed that support and so instigated a surprising revolution. He provided, as Ranke described the Magdalen case, 'the first occasion on which zealous members of the English Church defined obedience to the King in the same way in which his enemies also defined it'.[99] Or, as Aldworth put it, 'so long as we live up to them [the college's statutes], we obey the King'. The college's case, as Hough explained to Penn and to the king's commissioners, was about the defence both of a religion and of freehold rights. It was about material as well as spiritual concerns. If it is impossible to say which mattered most to him and his colleagues, this is because they themselves would have made no real distinction between the established church to which they belonged and the rights of property under the law.

To James and the Jacobites, the arch-villain was Sunderland who certainly played a chief part in devising and carrying out many of James's policies. As to Magdalen, he failed early on to make the fellows' reasonable objections to Anthony Farmer known to the king, nor, surprisingly, does he seem to have carried out his own enquiries about Farmer: a good example of the danger to the politician of relying on local and unsubstantiated knowledge. It is conceivable, as his biographer suggests, that he felt distaste for the task imposed on him, and that Thomas Smith when presenting the first petition in April 1687 mistook Sunderland's habitually haughty manner for hostility to the college. But on the unimpeachable evidence of Charles Hedges' private papers, he remained personally and deeply involved in the case, and he supported the incapacitation of the expelled fellows. It was apparently his suggestion that one of the new Catholic prelates should be appointed president.[100] His family connections with Magdalen

99. Leopold von Ranke, *A History of England Principally in the Seventeenth Century* (Oxford, 1875), iv. 336.

100. J. P. Kenyon, *Robert Spencer, Earl of Sunderland, 1641-1702* (London, 1958), 154; *Magdalen and James*, 242.

of which both his father and his son Robert had been members, and his own links with it through President Pierce who had been his private tutor, seem to have carried little weight with him. Yet in the Magdalen affair as in much else, including his clandestine links with William of Orange through his uncle Henry Sidney (one of the prince's chief supporters and the lover of the astute countess of Sunderland), the earl displayed inscrutable duplicity and ambiguity. He was far too intelligent to have been motivated merely by a love of power and wealth although he was certainly not averse from either. He was a gambler by taste and, in politics, by preference. The service of the dynamic James required apparent extremism to survive in office: Sunderland's need to outbid the Anglican Hyde family for James's favour led to his alliance with the 'dévots' at Court (principally Melfort and Petre) whom, given James's preferences, he could not control. His own 'conversion' to Catholicism was simply a political move. On the other hand, Thomas Smith was not alone in thinking that Sunderland's policies were designed to 'embarrass the King's affairs, and render him more odious to his Protestant subjects'. In his own defence, Sunderland claimed to have played only a small part in the ecclesiastical commission and to have defended the college 'for a good while'; 'hundreds of times' he had 'begged of the King never to grant Mandates' or to alter church affairs: it was others, presumably Petre and the Catholic 'enthusiasts', who prevailed on James 'against his own sense'.[101] From September 1688 he was pressing for concessions to Anglican interests, including the restoration of Magdalen, cynically oblivious of the fact that it was his own policies which had aroused so much opposition and now made hasty concessions necessary. His dismissal by the disillusioned king on 27 October, by making him the last and least innocent of James's victims, later helped him to ease his way back into the service of William and Mary. Back in England and a Protestant once again, he declared in 1691: 'My greatest misfortune has been to be thought the promoter of those things I opposed and detested'.[102] There was

---

101. Smith's Diary, 19 Jan. [1688]; and Sunderland's defence, *Magdalen and James*, 235, 267.

102. *DNB* (Spencer, Robert, 2nd earl of Sunderland).

just enough truth in this statement to carry conviction, and most of those who could have contradicted it were now in exile with James, or dead like Jeffreys and Cartwright, or like Hedges keeping a wise silence.

In his extremity, James received no assistance from Oxford in 1688, and when the whig Lord Lovelace took possession of the city on 5 December for William, 'he and his troops were welcomed by citizens and scholars alike'.[103] With very few exceptions the dons accepted the fact of the new regime even if they were soon to sabotage William's own policy of religious toleration. In Magdalen, the finances were not in their customarily good order. The bursars stated that

> being illegally depriv'd of their places & fellowships before they had given up their accounts to ye Audit, [they] did after their restoration upon ye 25th of October 1688 compleat that account [when it appeared that they had] in their hands in money... £309:11: 8 ob q d ... [and] that there remains a debt to ye College stock of £436:17:2 q^a c d.

Some disarray was to be expected, but the interesting point to emerge from the college's financial records is that several leases were sealed during the Catholic regime (in July, August and September 1688) and that many rents must have been paid as usual. There were difficulties over the payment of fines to renew leases. Of one such, to Mr Kendrick for lands in Brackley, Northamptonshire, the bursars noted that

> ...the reason why this fine was so small[£5], was because he had renew'd & pay'd a fine but 6 months before to the illegall usurpers of our places so that this fine is to be lookt upon as a punnishment on our part, & on his part as an acknowledgement that his former lease was invalid.[104]

There is no truth in the story, to be found first in Narcissus Luttrell's diary and sometimes repeated, that the Catholic fellows pawned much of the college plate before leaving.[105] A

---

103. Bennett, 'Loyalist Oxford,' 19.

104. Magdalen College MS, Draft Libri Computi, bursars' memorandum, n.d. [1688]; note, 17 Dec. 1688, to sealing of Mr Kendrick's lease.

105. Bloxam, *Register*, ii, p.clviii, n., citing Luttrell and correcting his story although without details.

'View' was taken of the plate on 7 November 1688 by Maynard, one of the bursars. Nothing was found missing from the time of the presidencies of Parker and Giffard; and the list of plate issued to Giffard on 4 May 1688 has a note dated 24 October [1688], the day before the restoration: 'y^c above mentioned plates (*sic*) wer[e] retur[n]'d by Mr. Presid.' It is signed 'J. Hough', as one president to another.[106] Earlier, between 16 and 18 October, the college seal in its box, all the keys, the vice-president's register and other vital records had all been returned along with the two silver candlesticks and 'the Bason' belonging to the chapel, and 'the Founder's Bowl'.[107] Nothing became the intruded fellows so much as their punctilious leaving of the college.

The college's finances were quickly repaired, and Magdalen prospered under Hough's presidency, as indeed he did when he became bishop of Oxford in 1690 and thus joined Mews on the episcopal bench. (That much-respected clerical statesman went on ruling his diocese effectively until his death at the age of eighty-nine in 1706.) In 1689 a brilliant generation of demies filled the large number of eighteen vacancies: it included the future essayist and statesman Joseph Addison, the combative tory churchman Henry Sacheverell, Hugh Boulter, later archbishop of Armagh, and Richard Smallbrooke, later bishop of Lichfield and Coventry. Yet while some of the fellows had successful public careers, the politics of the college remained resolutely tory and against the grain, to put it mildly, of national politics for many years. Hough's prestige and benevolence weighed much with a body of fellows most of whom disapproved of his support for William III's government. But he normally resided at Cuddesdon when he was not in London on his parliamentary duties and evidently took little part in college business. In 1699 he became bishop of Coventry and Lichfield, moved to his diocese and resigned the presidency

106. Magdalen College MS, CP2/38, Inventory of all the Colledge Goods, under 4 May, 24 Oct. 1688.
107. Magdalen College MS, CP2/29, Old Plate Book, under 16, 17, 18 Oct., 7 Nov. 1688.

in 1701. The fellows then elected the ailing John Rogers, a crypto-Jacobite who was commonly believed never to have taken the oath of allegiance. His successor in 1703, Thomas Bayley, was at least of non-juring sympathies under William III although he was prepared to acknowledge Queen Anne.[108] In neither these nor any subsequent elections at Magdalen did the Crown make the slightest attempt to intervene. The college had won a real independence in its freedom to choose its president and to run its own affairs. Oxford was to be caught up in the often fierce party strife of the next half-century, but as the politicians fought over the fertile pastures of patronage in the colleges and the university, the strong impression is that they steered clear of Magdalen — a place where resistance could appeal to a famous precedent.

Thomas Smith was more consistent and more honest than President Rogers. Immediately after the restoration, the college was made uncomfortable for him by the malicious behaviour towards him of some of the junior fellows; and in 1692, for refusing to swear the oaths of allegiance, he was removed from his fellowship by a majority vote. Hough bore him no ill will, indeed made several efforts to induce him to take the oaths, and they parted civilly with Smith wishing 'all happiness and prosperity to the College'. He went to live in the congenial household of Sir John Cotton, the grandson of the great collector. An avid collector himself, Smith led a productive scholarly life, publishing among other works a valuable catalogue of the Cottonian manuscripts and a life of the historian William Camden. He was a friend of Samuel Pepys, Thomas Hearne and Humphrey Wanley, and much in demand among his fellow scholars for his advice and learning. He died in 1710 at the age of seventy-one at the house of his friend Hilkiah Bedford, a non-juror like himself.[109]

Under the presidencies of Rogers, Bayley and Joseph Harwar (1706-22), the college certainly contained 'a considerable Jacobite element'. Some fellows resigned rather than swear allegiance to George I, and in 1715 a Jacobite agent on the run,

---

108. For Rogers, see Bennett, 'Against the Tide: Oxford under William III', *History of the University of Oxford*, v. 44; for Bayley, Wilson, *Magdalen College*, 216.

109. Bloxam, *Register*, iii. 182-204; *DNB*.

Colonel Owen, found safe refuge in Magdalen where he is said
to have hidden in the turret of the Grammar Hall.[110] This
Jacobitism gradually became more sentimental than active and
shaded off into toryism of an independent, 'country party' type.
But one former fellow paid for his Jacobitism with his life.
Robert Charnock, who was on leave of absence and probably
abroad when his name was 'crossed' in the Buttery Book, went
to serve with James's army in Ireland as a lieutenant in Colonel
John Parker's regiment of horse. By 1691 he was in London
where he became deeply implicated in a series of plots
culminating in Sir George Barclay's conspiracy to assassinate
King William. According to Macaulay, Charnock was foremost
among the conspirators 'in parts, in courage, and in energy'.
Arrested with his accomplices, he showed 'great presence of
mind, temper and judgement' at his trial in March 1696.
Macaulay thought that Charnock's fortitude eventually gave
way and that he offered to tell all that he knew of the Jacobites
and their plots in return for his life, but the evidence is by no
means certain: Burnet gives two accounts, one that Charnock
resisted all efforts to induce him to betray his friends, the other
that the king refused his confession because it would implicate
too many persons and imperil public security. In the end
Charnock gave nothing and nobody away. He was a
determined, ruthless man driven by his principles. He ordered
'a fine new coat to be hanged in, and was very particular on his
last day about the powdering and curling of his wig'.[111] But he
also left a long and impressive letter to an anonymous friend
explaining his motives in conspiring against 'the usurper', 'this
Perkin Warbeck of a King', and arguing that by virtue of James's
commission to levy war against William III and his adherents,
'the setting upon his [William's] person is justifyable as well by
the Lawes of the land...as by the Law of God'. He trusted his
friend to divulge his letter

> in a proper season, when the minds of men, grown more
> calme, shall be more susceptible of reason, and when it
> may be done without drawing more persecution upon thos

110. Wilson, *Magdalen College*, 217.
111. See Macaulay, *History*, v. 28, 118-21; *DNB* (Charnock).

honest men, who ly under the jealosy and suspition of the present governement.[112]

He died a traitor's death at Tyburn on 18 March 1696.

By a curious twist not uncommon in a time of extreme shifts of opinion, the political views of Henry Fairfax which had been poles apart from Charnock's in 1687-8, were probably not far from the latter's when he met his death. Fairfax was rewarded by the new regime in 1689 with the deanery of Norwich, but he evidently regarded this as much less than his due even when held with his Magdalen fellowship and the rectorship of Tubney in Oxfordshire. The account given of him by Humphrey Prideaux, then a prebendary of the cathedral who succeeded him as dean, begins with the relatively mild observation that Fairfax was 'good for nothing but his pipe and his pot'. But two years later he is drinking 'without measure'; he is 'this horrid sot we have got for our Dean'. In business, 'he acts by noe rules of justice, honesty, civility, or good manners...[and] nothing will satisfy him but to be an absolute king over us'. He never comes to the sacrament or looks into a book, and his dismissed servants spread tales of his eccentric behaviour through the county.[113] His chief, almost his only companion, Nathaniel Hodges, also a prebendary, had a whig past as a former chaplain to the earl of Shaftesbury, but Prideaux had heard that 'those that seem fierce Republicarians are in reallity fierce Jacobites'. Fairfax was 'much in with the [Jacobite] party, without considereing that if they prevail they will take his deanery from him'. His grievance was that

> ...he hath not higher advancement, that a bishoprick was not given him to reward his meritts; for he thinks noe meaner of himself then that he was the person that put y[e] crown on this Kings head, and he hath y[e] vanity and folly to say soe.[114]

Generous allowance should be made for Prideaux's sharp pen and his hostility as a Williamite to Jacobites and 'Republicarians', but the picture remains of Fairfax, now nearly sixty, as

112. Macray, *Register*, iv. 136-47.

113. *Letters of Humphrey Prideaux to John Ellis, 1674-1722*, ed. E. M. Thompson (Camden Society, 1875), 150-1, 159-61.

114. Ibid. 156, 157, 164.

a disappointed man given to drink who was an embarrassment if not worse to his clerical brethren, and who flirted at least with the cause of the king whom he had opposed with such spirit in 1687. But he was evidently no activist in the mould of Charnock, and died still dean of Norwich in his bed in 1702.

Of James's servants Cartwright fled to France, joined the king at Saint-Germain and accompanied him on his invasion of Ireland. There, after resisting all attempts to convert him to Catholicism as he lay mortally ill with dysentery, he died in Dublin on 15 April 1689. Wright and his patron Jeffreys were the chief official scapegoats (in James's fortunate absence) for the fallen regime. Wright went into hiding, was captured in Old Bailey, and as indecisive legal proceedings against him were taking place, died in Newgate on 18 May 1689. A month earlier Jeffreys, his health undermined by drink and in great pain from the stone and rheumatism, had died in the Tower. Jenner tried to flee with the king to France in December 1688. Captured at Faversham with others including Bonaventure Giffard and Obadiah Walker, he suffered only relatively short imprisonment and dismissal from his judgeship; in due course he quietly resumed his practice at the bar, and died in 1707. Giffard was less fortunate and was held without trial for over a year in Newgate. Although successive governments apparently did not regard him as politically dangerous, he led an unsettled life for many years; but he continued undeterred to go about his priestly duties until his death at Hammersmith in 1734 in his ninety-second year. By direction of his will, his heart was sent to the English college at Douai.

Hough's life was equally long but far more obviously successful and peaceful. In 1702 he made what turned out to be a happy marriage to Letitia, the forty-three year-old widow of Sir Charles Lee of Billesley, Warwickshire, and was translated in 1717 to the see of Worcester. There, as at Lichfield, he was a notably generous benefactor, particularly in the rebuilding of the bishop's palace and of his own later residence, Hartlebury Castle. While at Magdalen he had repaired the Lodgings at his own expense; later he gave the splendid sum of £1000 to the college's New Building fund. He seems to have been interested in the arts, and was a friend of the Irish painter and collector Charles Jervas who wrote him a long and amusing letter in 1703 from Rome where he was attempting to buy one of Raphael's cartoons.[115] Hough's reputation for 'pleasantry, philanthropy and the social virtues' earned him much respect, including a tribute to his 'unsullied mitre' from Alexander Pope,[116] and he evidently did not believe in nursing grudges. There is an agreeable anecdote (which, if true, must date from 1696-8) of his staying at Althorp as Sunderland's guest, when the talk turned to the conversion of King Augustus II of Poland to Catholicism. When Sunderland remarked, drawing no doubt on his own spiritual experiences, that the king 'would be a good Protestant again' one day, Hough replied that he would rather the king 'continued a Papist still than disgrace the Protestant cause' by forfeiting his sincerity. It says much for both men that Hough's plain speaking made no difference to their relations or, as Hough recalled, to Sunderland's noble hospitality.[117] Hough was the model of a politically moderate and resident bishop. He died on 8 May 1743 at the age of ninety-two. The magnificent monument to him in Worcester Cathedral by Roubiliac records his heroic resistance to the king's commissioners when, as a later memorialist and fellow of the college put it, he 'spoke and acted as a freeman of England, whose rights are established by law', and as a good subject 'trained in the best principles of allegiance to his Sovereign, submission to the laws, and a dutiful regard to the constituted authorities'.[118]

The struggle between Magdalen and James II, like the Revolution of which it formed a part, involved high principles and important issues along with men's self-interest, skilful as well as unwise management, and much chance and paradox. In holding President Hough in affectionate memory we should not forget the fellows and demies who supported him and were restored with him, including Thomas Smith, whose conscience took him along a different path. Three centuries later, it is also

---

115. Jervas to Hough, 24 Feb. N.S. 1703, in 'Table Talk…of Hough', 403-6. Hough's portrait was painted two or three times by Jervas, as well as by Kneller.
116. *Sermons and Charges by Hough*, ed. Russell, xxix; Wilmot, *Hough* 72.
117. 'Table Talk…of Hough', 392.
118. *Sermons and Charges by Hough*, ed. Russell, xxi.

'a proper season', in the Jacobite Charnock's phrase, to remember generously President Giffard and the intruded fellows whose possession of the college must have promised much to them and was to be so brief and unrewarding.

THE 'INTRUDED' PRESIDENT AND FELLOWS

*

LAURENCE BROCKLISS

To fill the places of the fellows who were expelled by James II's commissioners or later extruded by President Giffard, thirty fellows were appointed in their stead. All of these would be expelled in turn along with Giffard himself, with the exception of two who had apparently already left the college by 25 October.[1] The new admissions began on the very day the original fellows were expelled. On 16 November 1687 James's commissioners re-admitted a former fellow, William Joyner, who had resigned in 1645, and made three new elections: Job Allibon(e), Samuel Jenefar (or Ginever) and Thomas Higgons. The last two were demies who had agreed to serve under President Parker.[2] There was then a hiatus until January when eleven further fellows were admitted in response to a royal mandate of 31 December. Six were admitted on 9 January : Richard Compton, Thomas Fairfax, Philip Lewis, Alexander Cotton, Thomas G(u)ildford and Austin or Ambrose Belson; four more on 11 January : John Dryden, George Plowden, Lawrence Wood and John Ross(e); and one, John Christmas, on 30 January. The college received another royal mandate to appoint a fresh batch of fellows on 24 February. As a result six were elected on 2 March : Thomas or James Clerke, Robert

---

1. The Visitor expelled thirty fellows on 25 October. The list included the former fellow turned papist, Robert Charnock: see Bloxam, *Magdalen and James*, 265, list of names on the Buttery Book 20 October 1688; and Plate 4.

2. *Magdalen and James*, 207-8. The commissioners had a royal mandate to appoint a further six fellows, including another demy, Charles Goring, but no-one else appeared before them.

3. *Magdalen and James*, 225-31. Fairfax and Wood had already been nominated by the king in November, but they were included again on the list of 31 December. The king had originally asked the bishop of Oxford to admit twelve new fellows. One of the number, Edward Meredith, a London Jesuit, never presented himself.

Chetleborough or Chettleborrow, Francis Hungate, John Denham, Stephen Gallaway or Galloway and John Woolhouse; Charles Brockwell on 5 March; and Thomas Constable on 16 March. Thereafter until the appointment of President Giffard on 31 March, there was only one more election: that of Richard Short (exact date unknown), subsequent to the receipt of a royal mandate of 14 March.[4] On 4 June Giffard was granted by the crown 'full and sole power of nominating and admitting all such persons as you alone shall judge qualified according to the Statutes of the Founder'. The new president used this exceptional power on six occasions, securing the admission of Robert Jones and Edward Bertwisal (real name Hawarden) on 5 July, of Andrew Giffard (his brother), John Ward and John Harding or Hawarden on 9 July, and of Ralph Claiton (usually Clayton) on 7 October.[5]

The intruded fellows fall into three groups. The first consists of six fellows about whom nothing certain is known beyond the fact of their election and subsequent expulsion.[6] In some cases their surnames suggest that they were the scions of gentry recusant families. Francis Hungate, for instance, was presumably related to the Catholic Hungates of Saxton in Yorkshire. Arguably, he was the offspring of Sir Francis Hungate Bt., for the latter definitely had a second son of the same name who died on 27 October 1724.[7] Conclusive evidence, however, is impossible to come by. If the Magdalen fellow was the son of the baronet, then he was also the *Franciscus* Hungat, *Anglus*, who matriculated in medicine at Leiden in March 1687, aged 23.[8] Others in the group, on the

4. *Magdalen and James*, 238-40. The original mandate made nine nominations but one John Austin Bernard, MA, was never admitted.

5. *Magdalen and James*, 244-5, 247; Magdalen College MS 730(b), Vice-President's Register, *sub* 4 June; Magdalen College MS, Battels Book 1687-9, week commencing 6 October: 'Radulphus Claiton admissus est verus et perpetuus huius collegii socius 7 oct. 1688'; Bloxam does not record Claiton's election and wrongly transcribes his name as Clacton from the Buttery Book list of 20 October.

6. Clerke, Galloway, Guildford, Harding, Hungate, and Wood. Guildford and Wood are described as papists in a letter written by William Sherwin, university bedell, on 8 Jan. 1688; *Magdalen and James*, 231-2.

7. J. Foster, *Pedigrees of Yorkshire Families* (3 vols., London, 1884), i. *sub* Hungate of Saxton.

8. R. W. Innes Smith, *English-Speaking Students of Medicine at the*

other hand, offer no immediate indication of their identity. The origins of Stephen Galloway, for instance, remain totally obscure. Was he a Catholic Scotsman whose family had come south and had gained an *entrée* to James's Court? Was he a relation of the twenty-four year old John Galloway of Scotland who became an extra-licentiate of the Royal College of Physicians in 1672-3 and two years later enrolled at Leiden? This would seem plausible, if he was, as Bloxam maintains, the Roman Catholic physician of Red-Lion Square, London, whose death was recorded in the *Gentleman's Magazine* for 1731. But even this connection must remain putative. As in the case of Francis Hungate, there is no evidence that Stephen Galloway of Magdalen was a student of physic. If the Magdalen fellow was the London physician, however, we also know that in later life he married Elizabeth Turbeville and in 1706 had a son Edward who became a Jesuit in 1724.[9]

The second group comprises nine fellows who were reared ostensibly in the Anglican faith and had attended Oxford or Cambridge prior to becoming fellows of Magdalen.[10] At least one, John Christmas, had taken Anglican orders and others had or had had relations in the ministry. The demy, Thomas Higgons, for instance, was the grandson of a parson and the nephew of the Dean of Durham.[11] Most or all of the group were sons of gentlemen, and Higgons was the son of a knight. Their education prior to attending Oxford or Cambridge remains generally unknown but it can be assumed that they had either been privately tutored or introduced to the Latin and Greek humanities at a local grammar school. Christmas had attended Sudbury grammar school while John Dryden, the second son of the poet, and Thomas Woolhouse had been entrusted to the

---

University of Leyden (Edinburgh, 1932), 123. Foster, *Pedigrees*, says the son of the baronet was an MD.

9. W. Munk, *The Roll of the Royal College of Physicians of London* (4 vols., London, 1878-1955), i. 366; Innes Smith, 91; *Gentleman's Magazine* 1(1731), 34; G. Holt, *St Omers and Bruges Colleges, 1593-1773. A Biographical Dictionary*, Catholic Record Society xlix (London, 1979), 110; G. Holt, *The English Jesuits 1650-1829. A Biographical Dictionary*, Catholic Record Society xlxx (London, 1984), 98.

10. Brockwell, Chetleborough, Christmas, Denham, Dryden, Higgons, Jenefar, Joyner and Woolhouse.

11. *Magdalen and James*, 229, n.9; *DNB* (Higgons, Sir Thomas and Bevil).

care of the famous Dr Busby at Westminster. Woolhouse, born in 1666, had been a king's scholar on the foundation in 1681. From there he had gone to Trinity College, Cambridge, in 1684, first as a pensioner and then from 1 May 1685 as a scholar. Dryden was virtually his contemporary. Born in 1667 or 1668, he, too, had been a king's scholar at Westminster (from 1682) and had proceeded to Oxford in 1685. Elected to Christ Church he never took up his scholarship but went instead to University College under the eye of the Catholic Master, Obadiah Walker.[12] Dryden, Woolhouse and Higgons were in their early twenties. The others were more mature. Denham, Jenefar, Chetleborough, Christmas and Brockwell had all taken their BA in the years 1679-1684, while William Joyner was born as early as 1622.[13]

How many of these 'Anglican' fellows were converts to Rome is impossible to tell. Some, perhaps the majority, never left the faith of their fathers at all. This was surely true of Jenefar and Higgons who were expelled from their fellowships on 25 October but reinstated as demies. Had they been apostates, this action on the part of the bishop of Winchester would be incomprehensible.[14] Jenefar and Higgons should rather be seen as obedient tories. Some, on the other hand, had definitely converted to Rome before their appointment to Magdalen. John Christmas had suddenly 'gone over' some time in 1687. Rector of Cornard Parva in Suffolk from 1686, he had contrived to continue to hold the living (worth £40) after his

12. G. F. Russell Barker and Alan H. Stenning, *The Record of Old Westminsters* (2 vols., London, 1928), i. 288-9; ii. 1022; J. Welch, *The List of the Queen's Scholars of St Peter's College, Westminster, Admitted on the Foundation since 1663 and of such as have been thence elected to Christ Church Oxford and Trinity College Cambridge* ed. C. B. Phillimore (London, 1852), 203-4; W. W. Rouse Ball and J. A. Venn, *Admissions to Trinity College Cambridge* (5 vols., London, 1911-16), *sub* Woolhouse; *Magdalen and James*, 228, n.4.

13. J. Foster, *Alumni Oxonienses 1500-1714* (4 vols., Oxford, 1891-2), *sub* Brockwell (Magdalen Hall 1684), Denham (Magdalen 1676), Jenefar (New, Wadham and Magdalen 1681), and Joyner (BA 1640); J. Venn and J. A. Venn, *Alumni Cantabrigienses. Part I to 1751* (4 vols., Cambridge, 1922-7), *sub* Chettleburgh (Corpus Christi MA 1683), and Christmas (Christ's 1683-4). Also, J. Peile, *Biographical Register of Christ's College, 1505-1905, and of the Earlier Foundation, God's House, 1448-1505* (2 vols., Cambridge, 1910-13), ii. 77; W. J Harrison, *Notes on the Masters, Fellows etc. of Clare* (Cambridge, 1953), 41: Chetleborough was a Borage Fellow at Clare 1683-8.

14. Macray, *Register*, iv. 151-2.

conversion thanks to a royal dispensation.[15] John Dryden's change of heart seems, like his father's, to have come gradually. As early as 1682, at the age of fourteen, he must have had some doubts. In the middle of that year his mother Elizabeth was compelled to write to Dr Busby apologizing for her son's absence from the Abbey and promising he would go to church on Sundays and holidays. By 1685 his conversion was complete. It was for this reason that he went up to University College rather than Christ Church.[16] As recent converts, of course, neither Christmas nor Dryden had had to suffer for their change of allegiance. A far braver soul was William Joyner. An Oxford man born and bred, Joyner had been a demy and then a fellow of Magdalen from 1642 to 1645. Turning to Rome, he resigned his fellowship and condemned himself to a life of poverty. Whether he went abroad during the Interregnum is unknown but he was back in England during the Exclusion crisis. Banned like other popish recusants from living within ten miles of London, he retired to his brother's house at Horspath outside Oxford. Even there he was not allowed to rest at peace, for the vice-chancellor of the university issued a warrant for his arrest and had him incarcerated (temporarily) for refusing to take the Oath of Supremacy. Joyner never took orders in the Roman Church. According to Wood, he relied on charity, receiving on several occasions funds from his old college.[17]

After their expulsion this second group seem to have gone their separate ways. Joyner once more became a recluse, and died in 1706. At one stage he lived at Ickford in Buckinghamshire.[18] Jenefar, at least in Anne's reign, joined the majority of his tory countrymen and became reconciled to the regime. From 1703-1715 he was the vicar of Horndon-on-the-

---

15. Macray, *Register*, iv. 152-5; Venn, *sub nomine*, says Christmas held the living until 1689.

16. Welch, 204. Dryden's father did not convert until 1686. J. A. Winn, *John Dryden and His World* (London, 1987), 415, is not convinced that Dryden jnr did study under Walker. What is certain is that the young Dryden did not matriculate and was not therefore forced to take an oath supporting the Anglican religion.

17. Macray, *Register*, iii. 185-6; and iv. 152; Wood, *Life and Times*, ii. 427, 433.

18. Wood, *Life and Times*, iii. 486, 491.

Hill, Essex.[19] Brockwell seems to have become a historian, translating Pufendorf's *History of Sweden* in 1702 and publishing an account of the first three years of George I's reign in 1716-17.[20] Others remained committed to the Jacobite cause and fled abroad. Christmas went abroad and was admitted to the English college at Douai in July 1690. He returned to England in 1693 and joined the English Mission, dying in Oxford, possibly an Anglican again, in 1743.[21] Dryden set himself up in self-imposed exile in Italy, becoming deputy to his brother who was a chamberlain in the household of pope Clement XI. Throughout the 1690s he pursued a literary career writing plays, travelogues and translating Juvenal's *Satires*. He eventually died of a fever in 1703 after touring Sicily and Malta with a Mr Cecil.[22]

By far the most exotic career was that of Thomas Higgons. In 1689 he resigned his demyship and along with his brother, Bevil, a Middle Temple lawyer, went into exile at the court of James II. A few years, later, however, the brothers returned to England, where Thomas became involved in the 1695-6 plot to assassinate William III, presumably through a continued acquaintance with his Magdalen colleague and leading Jacobite conspirator, Charnock. Fortunately, Bevil acted as a moderating influence on the former demy and Thomas' attachment to the conspiracy was peripheral. Nevertheless both brothers were arrested, questioned and temporarily imprisoned. Once released Thomas went abroad again and became a permanent fixture at Saint-Germain. In the following years his political fortunes rose. Eventually in 1713, now a knight like his father, he became secretary of state to the Old

19. Macray, *Register*, iv. 152; Jenefar resigned his demyship in 1689.

20. Ch. Brockwell, *A Chronological History of Great Britain. An Abstract of the First to the Third Year of the Reign of King George* (London, 1716-17). He also wrote *The Natural and Political History of Portugal* (London, 1726). It is just possible that the historian was another Charles Brockwell. The British Library catalogue describes the historian as an alumnus of Catharine Hall, Cambridge, but this is definitely wrong. The Cambridge Ch. Brockwell matriculated in 1716-17 (see Venn and Venn, *sub nomine*).

21. G. Anstruther, *The Seminary Priests. A Dictionary of the Secular Priests of England and Wales 1558-1850* (4 vols., Great Wakering, 1969-77), ii. 254. On the English college at Douai, see below pp. 89-94.

22. Macray, *Register*, iv. 156-7; Winn, 480-2, 626, n. John Dryden was related to the Cecils of Burghley House through his mother.

Pretender at Bar in Lorraine. Throughout he remained loyal to his Anglican background. He died as he had lived, a Jacobite tory.[23]

The third and final group comprises fifteen fellows and President Giffard who gained their formal education, not in England, but in one of the colleges founded on the continent for the sons of English Catholics.[24] In the course of the late-sixteenth and early-seventeenth centuries some half a dozen English colleges were established in Catholic countries to educate the sons of recusant gentlemen.[25] Their primary function was to provide priests for the English Mission but they also offered a religiously sound alternative to Oxford and Cambridge for elder sons who would one day be the lay protectors of the old religion in the shires. Of the foundations, only two, Douai and St Omer, were of any importance in terms of their size, the first run by English seculars and the second by the Jesuits. In the period 1660 to 1688 there were 80 to 90 students at Douai and 120 to 180 at St Omer, while the other colleges seldom boasted a dozen.[26] It is scarcely surprising, then, to find that all but four of the sixteen fellows in the group

23. *DNB* (Higgons, Bevil); Sir Charles Petrie, *The Jacobite Movement* (London, 1959), 467; Mq. of Ruvigny, *The Jacobite Peerage* (Edinburgh, 1904), 191, 207, 215, 219. Another member of the group may have followed the Stuarts into exile. Macray (iv. 161) identifies John Woolhouse with the FRS, J. T. Woolhouse, d. 1734, who was oculist to James II at Saint-Germain and about whose early life nothing is known: see *DNB* (Woolhouse). I am not convinced: seventeenth and eighteenth century oculists were low-grade medical practitioners who passed their 'mystery' from father to son and were not known for their academic training; admittedly J. T. Woolhouse published in Latin.

24. Allibone, Belson, Bertwisal/Hawarden, Clayton, Constable, Compton, Cotton, Fairfax, Giffard (Andrew and Bonaventure), Lewis, Jones, Plowden, Ross, Short and Ward. Lewis and Ross have been placed in this group for convenience. Lewis was a Catholic priest working in England in the 1640s but nothing is known of his education; Ross was the son of an exiled royalist brought up at the German monastery of Fulda and then trained at the English college of Rome: see Anstruther, iii. 132-3, 190.

25. A. C. F. Beales, *Education under Penalty* (London, 1963) 115-157; P. Guilday, *The English Catholic Refugees on the Continent* (London, 1914), 63-120, 307-345.

26. Holt, *St Omers and Bruges Colleges*, p. 3; *Douai College Documents 1639-1794*, ed. P. R. Harris, Catholic Record Society xliii (London, 1972), 19-32, 40-3 (sample lists of alumni 1661, 1663, 1668); *Registers of the English College at Valladolid 1589-1682*, ed. E. Henson, Catholic Record Society xxx (London, 1930), xxiii-xxxiii, *passim*. There is no detailed secondary history of the Douai foundation, but on St Omer, see H. Chadwick, *St Omers to Stonyhurst* (London, 1962).

had attended these two institutions. Among the exceptions was John Ward (later a college bursar), who under the pseudonym of Rogers was admitted to the English college at Valladolid in October 1656 to read theology, after first studying philosophy at the University of Granada.[27]

Understandably the majority of the group were the sons of confirmed recusants. Attendance at an English college abroad was illegal, and to send a child overseas to be educated was an act of defiance requiring courage and forethought. Nevertheless, at least one of the group was born to Protestant parents. Job Allibone, born in 1638, was the third son of Job Allibone of Spawforth, Yorks. He and his elder brother, Richard, later a judge in King's Bench, were sent to Douai in 1652, Richard arriving in March and Job in late December. At this date Job Allibone senior and his wife Margaret, *née* Chamber, were definitely both Protestants and Job junior was at best a recent convert. He is described in the Douai college records as 'nuper in fide Catholica instructa.'[28] Even thirteen years later, when Job was about to leave the college and go on the Mission, his father was still a Protestant. In a list of students taking the missionary oath in 1665, Job was described as 'natus haereticis parentibus, huius tamen mater duobus abhinc annis haeresim abjuravit in Catholicam Ecclesiam aggregata'.[29] But if the Allibones were brought up as Protestants, what could have induced their parents to give them a Catholic education? Perhaps an explanation lies in the troubled years of the Interregnum. Arguably, Allibone senior thought it a lesser evil to give his sons a papist upbringing than to expose them to the rampant sectarianism rife in the Puritan-controlled colleges of Oxford and Cambridge.

27. *English College at Valladolid*, 167.

28. *Douai Diaries 1598-1654*, ed. E. H. Burton and J. L. Williams, Catholic Record Society x and xi (2 vols., London, 1910-11), ii. 516, 522. The principals of the Douai college kept a detailed diary for two centuries after the college's foundation. This is a unique record of an early-modern educational institution which is a mine of information about the students, student-life and the curriculum. Unfortunately, the diary is missing for the second half of the seventeenth century. Were it extant, it is possible that a number of the fellows in the first group would have been found to have studied at Douai. All that survives for this crucial period is a number of lists of alumni from different years.

29. *Douai College Documents 1639-1794*, 34.

Nearly all of this final group had been destined for a life in the church. On their admission to Magdalen, ten were secular priests, two, Thomas Fairfax and Alexander Cotton, were Jesuits (although the latter was apparently not yet ordained), and one, Thomas Constable, an Anglo-Benedictine.[30] A fourteenth fellow, Richard Compton, had definitely begun to prepare for the priesthood, for like Cotton and the secular priest George Plowden he had moved from St Omer to the Jesuits' English seminary at Rome. Compton, however, did not become a priest until 1701 after he had returned to Rome in 1699.[31] Only Richard Short, son of a Catholic licentiate of the Royal College of Physicians, was clearly intended for a different career. Transferred from Douai to Magdalen on completing his humanities, Short returned to the Low Countries on his expulsion to study philosophy before proceeding to Montpellier to read for a medical degree. Graduating in 1694 he next went off to Italy to perfect his medical knowledge, then returned to England via Paris and was admitted to the Royal College of Physicians in turn in 1696.[32]

On the whole members of this third group of fellows were considerably older than the fellows educated in England. Twelve out of the sixteen were born between *c.* 1637 and *c.* 1655, and seven were in their forties when they entered the college. The oldest was probably Alexander Cotton, who had been sent by his parents to Douai in 1649 at the early age of eleven.[33] In consequence, most of the priests had had

---

30. Cotton became a Jesuit in 1656, Fairfax in 1675: see Holt, *The English Jesuits*, 71, 90. Constable joined the English congregation of Benedictines at Douai in 1649: see H. M. Birt, *Obit Book of the English Benedictines (1600-1912)* (Edinburgh, 1913), 73-4, where he is called Thomas Augustine.

31. *The Responsa Scholarum of the English College, Rome. Part II 1622-85*, ed. A. Kenny, Catholic Record Society lv (London, 1963), 551. *Liber Ruber of the English College Rome. I. Nomina aluminorum 1631-1783*, ed. W. Kelly, Catholic Record Society xl (London, 1943), 82, 96, 129-30. Plowden and Compton were contemporaries at Rome; Plowden was there 1670-7, Compton 1671-4. Cotton had attended the seminary in the mid-1650s. Pupils at St Omer seem to have been free to move to Rome to train for the priesthood, and there seems to have been no pressure on alumni to become Jesuits.

32. Macray, *Register*, iv. 160; Munk, ii. 516-7.

33. Cotton had an elder brother, George, also a Jesuit and active on the Mission in the London area 1670-96: see Holt, *English Jesuits*, 71. The Cottons were a Surrey recusant family which suffered for its faith during the Civil War. On arriving at Rome in 1655, Cotton claimed to be destitute: 'Conditio

considerable experience on the English Mission before James came to the throne, so were unlikely to have been carried away with thoughts of rapidly converting the country to Rome. As was the custom, they had administered to the Catholic faithful in the areas where they had lived as children. The Giffards were (and still are) a gentry family living near Wolverhampton. Andrew, the younger brother of the president, was born in 1646, the son of another Andrew. Sent to Douai probably in the late 1650s he seems to have left the college in 1667, along with his more illustrious brother. Where and when he was ordained is unknown but for many years prior to James's accession he was on the mission in his home county of Staffordshire. It was only the Catholic resurgence after 1685 that drew him out of his rural retreat and into the maelstrom of Catholic proselytism in the capital. In 1686 he was priest in charge of the notorious Lime Street Chapel.[34]

Arguably, too, this third group of fellows was better educated than its Oxford- or Cambridge-trained counterparts. Theoretically, all the intruded fellows had been subjected to a similar process of acculturation. Both the Oxford and Cambridge Bachelors of Arts and the graduates of Douai or St Omer should have been competent classical scholars and philosophers. In the course of their education they ought to have been introduced to the best Greek and Latin authors, learnt how to write and speak Latin fluently, and spent their final years studying an amalgam of Aristotelian, scholastic and contemporary logic, ethics, metaphysics and natural science.[35] In reality, the English-

parentum et mea ut nobili loco ortorum tenuis satis, a Parliamentariis quippe et Haereticis hisce temporibus fidei causa attenuata'; *Responsa Scholarum*, 551. Both Constable and Belson may have been older than Cotton. Belson matriculated at Douai in 1647 but his date of birth, like Constable's, is unknown: see J. F. Knox (ed.), *The First and Second Diaries of the English College Douai* (London, 1888), 81.

34. *Douai College Documents*, 22, 28, 32, 109; Macray, *Register*, iv. 157-8. On the Lime Street chapel, formerly Fishmongers' Hall, see Miller, *Popery and Politics*, 246-7. Its notoriety arose from the fact that it was the first Catholic chapel opened in London in James's reign.

35. In the third quarter of the seventeenth century the study of philosophy and the universities and colleges of France and England was in a state of transition: see L. W. B. Brockliss, 'Philosophy Teaching in France 1600-1740', *History of Universities*, 1 (1981), 131-68; J. Gascoygne, 'The Universities and the Scientific Revolution: the case of Newton and Restoration Cambridge', *History of Science*, xxiii (1985), 391-434.

trained fellow may have had serious lacunae in his knowledge.

English university education throughout the seventeenth and eighteenth centuries was notoriously varied in quality. Students went up to Oxford or Cambridge in their early teens after studying classical grammar with a private tutor or at a local school. Once there they entered a college and studied rhetoric and philosophy for three to four years under the guidance of one of the fellows. Just as today the fellows acted as personal tutors and students largely worked on their own. Students were asked to read selected texts which they then went away to peruse on their own, prior to a discussion in their tutor's rooms. Unlike today, however, there was little support teaching. University or college lectures for undergraduates were virtually non-existent and never compulsory. Obviously the success of such a system depended totally on the assiduity of tutor and pupil. It could easily be abused, and a student could emerge after a perfunctory examination scarcely more knowledgeable than on his arrival. Gibbon's strictures against the system in the mid-eighteenth century at Magdalen may have been exaggerated but not totally unfair. It is hard not to feel that the tutorial system was inadequately structured given the youth of the undergraduate body.[36]

At Douai and St Omer, on the other hand, the course in the humanities and philosophy was more carefully structured, following the model developed at the University of Paris in the first half of the sixteenth century and honed to perfection in the colleges of the Society of Jesus. To begin with, students usually entered the college at a much earlier stage in their intellectual development. While still normally in their early teens on arrival, they usually knew little more than the rudiments of Latin grammar, so there was little differential in levels of attainment on arrival. Secondly and more importantly, the course in the humanities and philosophy was divided into a

36. E. Gibbon, *Memoirs of My Life*, ed. G. A. Bonnard (London, 1966), ch.3. The development of the tutorial system is explored in M. Curtis, *Oxford and Cambridge in an Age of Transition 1558-1642* (Oxford, 1959), 78-125. One of the first Oxford colleges to attempt to exercise some form of control over the anarchic system was Christ Church from the beginning of the eighteenth century: see P. Quarrie, 'The Christ Church Collection Books', in *The History of the University of Oxford: vol. v: The Eighteenth Century*, ed. L. S. Sutherland and L. G. Mitchell (Oxford, 1986), 493-512.

series of graded stages, each with its own prescribed curriculum intended to be taught in a year. Instruction at each stage was given in classes. For some four to five hours every day of the week except Sunday all the students at the same stage in the course would be closeted with a professor who would subject his charges to a relentless round of dictations and written and verbal exercises. Even once classroom teaching was over for the day, the students would continue to be closely supervised. The students would retire to their common room where they would prepare for the next day's lessons under the watchful eye of their moral supervisor. Those who emerged from a course in the arts at Douai or St Omer might not have been original minds but they would certainly have been successfully drilled in the linguistic and logical tools of scholarly discourse. Their presence in Magdalen guaranteed that the intruded fellows contained a hardcore of skilful debaters and controversialists for the future.[37]

Furthermore, most of the fellows educated abroad had not just completed their arts course but perfected their studies and gone on to take a three- or four-year course in theology. They were not then ordinary members of the English mission but the *crème de la crème*. Douai was a university town, and alumni of the English college probably attended theology lectures in the university faculty. Job Allibone, for instance, finished his arts course in 1658. He remained at Douai, however, until 1666, first teaching the humanities (including the rhetoric class in 1661 and 1663), and then studying moral and scholastic theology.[38] St Omer, however, had no university and the college itself offered no theology tuition. In consequence, the Jesuits transferred their best pupils to other establishments which were better equipped. As we have seen, some pupils went off to the English college at Rome, but more commonly, especially where a student was earmarked to join the Society,

---

37. A general introduction to the teaching of the arts in France is given in L. W. B. Brockliss, *French Higher Education in the Seventeenth and Eighteenth Centuries. A Cultural History* (Oxford, 1987), esp. chs. 2 and 3. The genesis of the system is described in G. Codina Mir, *Aux sources de la pédagogie des Jésuites: le modus parisiensis* (Rome, 1968). The importance of surveillance is emphasized in G. Snyders, *La Pédagogie en France aux XVIIᵉ et XVIIIᵉ siècles* (Paris, 1965), Bk.I, pt.i.

38. *Douai College Documents*, 21, 26, 34.

pupils from St Omer moved to the local Jesuit novitiates at Watten and Liège. Thomas Fairfax's educational odyssey can be taken as typical. Born in 1655 he left St Omer in 1675 to join the Jesuit Order at Watten. For the next three years he presumably gained a deeper acquaintance with the arts before moving to Liège to re-take his philosophy course and study theology. His studies complete in 1683 he was ordained at the end of the year, then moved to Ghent to do his statutory apprenticeship as a Jesuit out in the field.[39] The Jesuits' concern to train their theologians themselves arose from fears of doctrinal pollution. Catholicism in late-seventeenth century Europe was as rent by divisions as Protestantism, most of all over the relative roles of free will and divine grace in meritorious action. The Jesuits under the influence of their late-sixteenth century theologian, Molina, laid the emphasis on free will. The Dominicans, on the other hand, believed that Molinism was an affront to the dignity of God, while the austere Augustinian followers of Jansen, bishop of Ypres, were eventually declared to be heretics for supposedly denying the existence of free will altogether.[40]

Allibone and Fairfax were representative figures among the fellows educated on the continent. President Giffard, on the other hand, had a unique intellectual pedigree. Alone of the group, indeed almost alone among the English secular clergy in the reign of James II, Giffard was a doctor of theology of Paris, the most prestigious Catholic faculty in Europe.[41] His educational biography can be charted in some detail. Born supposedly in 1642 he was christened Joseph, not Bonaventure, and it is under this name that he first appears in the Douai records studying philosophy in 1661. Two years later he was a

39. Holt, *English Jesuits*, 90. Macray, *Register*, iv. 150, says Fairfax was a DD of Trier but Holt does not mention this.

40. A useful if biased laymen's introduction to the quarrel is B. Pascal, *Lettres provinciales* [originally 1656-7], esp. the first four and the last letters. Pascal was a Jansenist. The best secondary accounts are A. Adam, *Du mysticisme à la révolte. Les Jansénistes du XVIIe siècle* (Paris, 1968), and H. de Lubac, *Augustinianism and Modern Theology*, Eng. trans. L. Sheppard (London, 1963).

41. Admittedly, Giffard was not the only doctor in the group; Robert Jones had taken a DD at Douai on 25 Feb. 1686, while Compton is called doctor in the Buttery Book: J. Gillow, *A Literary and Biographical History or Bibliographical Dictionary of English Catholics from 1534* (5 vols., London, 1885-1902), v. 374-5, sub Pugh (Jones's alias); Magdalen College MS, Battels Book 1687-9.

student of theology, described as a gentleman 'magnae spei', and in 1666 at the age of twenty-five, obviously now ordained, he was pronounced ready to go on the mission as a 'iuvenis acris ingenii'.[42] It was at this moment that some sort of crisis must have occurred in the future president's life. In 1667 two confessors attached to the college, Thomas Shepherd (real name Prance) and Edward Lutton (real name Eldrington), came into bitter conflict with the principal, George Leyburn, by discouraging student priests from returning home and doing their duty. Among members of the college who supported this initiative was none other than Joseph Giffard. Presumably, for some reason or other, Giffard, too, was refusing to go on the Mission.[43] In Giffard's case the quarrel was resolved by his removal to Paris at the end of the year. He was accompanied to the capital by one of the other troublemakers, John Betham, to whom we are indebted for the following, somewhat sanitized, account of their departure:

In the year 1667 Mr Bonaventure Giffard and Mr John Betham both preists [*sic*] having ended their studies at ye English Colledg of Douay, were adverstised by Dr Leyburne then President of the said Colledge to prepare 'emselves to goe imediatly for ye mission of England: where-upon Mr John Betham desiring to passe some time in a Seminarie at Paris intreated Dr Leyburne to give leave for it, w^{ch} *he willingly granted* [my italics], and with all told him that Mr Bon: Giffard should accompany him if he pleasd. Mr Giffard readily embraced ye offer and some days after they both began their journey.[44]

Betham and Giffard arrived in Paris in October 1667 and for the next few months lived in a variety of improvised lodgings. In February 1668, however, they teamed up with an expatriate priest of means called Miles Pinkney (*alias* Thomas Carre), bought a house and announced the establishment of an English secular community in the city, later to be called St Gregory's

42. *Douai College Records*, 24, 27, 37.

43. Ibid. 38-9. On Prance, see Anstruther, ii. 254.

44. *The Register Book of St Gregory's College Paris 1667-1786*, ed. E. H. Burton, Catholic Record Society, xix (London, 1917), 101-2. For Betham (c. 1642-1709), see Gillow, i. 204-5.

College. Interestingly, one of the first members of this community, arriving in October 1668, was the peevish Edward Lutton, destined for a career as chaplain to a Paris convent of English nuns.[45] From their arrival, it would seem, Betham and Giffard attended lectures in the faculty of theology. By 1670 they had definitely decided to take a Paris degree, for in that year they sought and gained through the influence of another expatriate, the *abbé* Walter Montagu, an exemption from the requirement that graduands had studied philosophy at Paris.[46]

Becoming a Paris doctor was a lengthy and arduous process, as befitted the distinction which the title bestowed. Supplicants had first to follow a five-year course in philosophy and theology in the University's schools and take a Paris MA. They then had to gain the degrees of bachelor and licentiate in theology, which were taken with an interval of five years between them. Neither degree was bestowed as a mere formality. Candidates for the baccalaureate and licence had first to be orally examined by a panel of faculty doctors where they were asked to demonstrate their theological knowledge. Next they gave evidence of their dialectical skills by upholding a series of positions in a public debate. Prospective bachelors had to undergo only one *soutenance*, the *tentativa*, devoted to the theology of grace; licensiands underwent three: the Minor and Major Ordinary on the sacraments and church government, and the *Sorbonica* on the Incarnation. The *soutenance* was a test of stamina as well as skill. The *Sorbonica* lasted all day, from 6 am to 6 pm.[47]

Giffard, now called Bonaventure, took his Paris MA on 29 August 1671 and sustained his *tentativa* on 26 October.[48] Bachelors were supposed to prepare for their licence by two years of private study, so having taken the baccalaureate Giffard returned with Betham to Douai where the new

45. *St Gregory's Paris*, 102. Lutton died at Paris in 1713: see Anstruther, iii. 55-6.

46. Ibid. 103. Walter Montagu was the son of the Puritan first earl of Manchester and had converted to Catholicism in 1635.

47. Brockliss, *Higher Education*, 74. The requirements for the doctorate are laid down in the 1675 statutes: see P. Feret, *La Faculté de théologie de Paris. Epoque Moderne* (7 vols., Paris, 1900-12), iii. 476-89.

48. *St Gregory's Paris*, 103; Bibliothèque Nationale (Paris), MS Latin 9155, fo. 95, list of graduates in arts.

principal, John Leyburn, nephew of George, was clearly willing to bury the hatchet. For the next two years (1672-3) Giffard taught divinity, then once more took the road to the capital (still with Betham) to begin the next stage of his doctorate. The preliminary examination for the licence was conducted under the aegis of M. Gobillon, the *curé* of the Paris parish of Saint-Laurent, in July 1674, but it was not until 4 May 1676 that Giffard sustained his first public debate, the Major Ordinary. The following year he completed his licence examinations by sustaining his Minor Ordinary on 28 January and his *Sorbonica* on 13 August. He next duly appeared on the roll of licentiates in theology for 1678 and on 10 June of the same year 'Mr Giffard took his Doctors cap, Mr George Witham making ye Expectative and Aulik'.[49]

There can be no doubt that by the time Giffard went on the Mission in July 1678 he had a formidable education.[50] It is no surprise that in 1685 he was chosen by James II to be one of his preachers-in-ordinary, then in January 1688 to be (along with his former principal, John Leyburn) one of the four vicars-apostolic under the title of bishop of Madaura, and finally President of Magdalen on Parker's death the following March. Giffard's credentials were impeccable. He was an ideal figure to occupy a prominent place in the consolidation of English Catholicism.[51] Giffard, however, was certainly not over-whelmed by the sudden change in his fortunes with James's accession. Although he initially attempted to flee with the king in October 1688 and was caught and temporarily imprisoned, he never became a Jacobite exile tempted by the fantasy life of

---

49. *St Gregory's Paris*, 103-5; Bibliothèque Nationale, MS Latin 15440, p. 262, list of licentiates; *Douai College Documents*, 46 n, 70, 87. The *expectiva* and the *aulica* were formal speeches made when a doctor's degree was conferred. George Witham (1655-1725) became a Paris DD in 1689: for his future career, see *DNB* (Witham).

50. Giffard was back in Paris from April 1679 to July 1681. Unlike most of the seculars he fled from England at the height of the Exclusion crisis: *St Gregory's Paris*, 105-6.

51. In the reign of James II there were only two Paris DD's in England: Giffard and Betham; the latter was also a royal preacher. The only other Paris DD on the English Mission before their arrival was Francis Gage, MA in 1646 and licentiate in theology in 1654. Gage (1621-82) died as principal of Douai College: Gillow, ii. 354-6. None of the other three vicars-apostolic was as well educated as Giffard, although the former Douai principal, John Leyburn, was a Paris MA in 1646: see Bibliothèque Nationale, MS Latin 9154, fo. 76.

Saint-Germain. Instead on his release he returned to the relative poverty and insecurity of life on the English Mission. Until 1703 he occupied the position which he had been given in 1688 as vicar-apostolic to the midland district; and he probably lived pseudo-anonymously at the family home near Wolverhampton. In 1703, however, he became vicar-apostolic to the London district on the death of John Leyburn, and it was in the capital that he ended his days in 1734.[52]

Giffard's steadfastness in his duty once the bad days returned again was generally mirrored in the behaviour of the other fellows educated abroad. Only three of the group seem to have returned immediately to the continent on James' 'abdication'. Richard Short and Edward Bertwisal/Hawarden both went back to Douai, the first to complete his course in the arts, the second to teach theology and take his DD. George Plowden (the former vice-president), on the other hand, probably joined the Court-in-exile, for he died in the vicinity of Saint-Germain at Pontoise in 1694.[53] The rest of the group who were already ordained once more went on the Mission. Job Allibone (died 1709) was active in Yorkshire, Robert Jones in Sussex, and Ralph Clayton in Worcestershire. A number, like Bonaventure Giffard himself, eventually ended their days in London. Both Jones and Andrew Giffard died in the city in 1714, the first the ex-president's archdeacon, the second his brother's grand-vicar who had deliberately turned down the post of vicar-apostolic to the west in 1705. The Jesuit Thomas Fairfax died in the capital two years later after serving his Order all over the country. In 1690-1 he was attached to the Jesuit residence of St Mary which covered the southern midlands; he then moved north to his home territory of Yorkshire and joined the residence of St Michael; finally in 1714 he was called to the capital and entered the college of St Ignatius serving the home counties. For many their final resting place must have been the Catholic cemetery in St Pancras churchyard.[54]

52. Gillow, ii. 454-6. Betham, in contrast, did go into exile at Saint-Germain.

53. Holt, *English Jesuits*, 197.

54. Macray, *Register*, iv. 149, 157-159; *Douai College Documents*, 83, 87, 109; Gillow, v, 374-5; *The Letter Book of Lewis Sabran, S.J. (Rector of St Omers College) October 1713 to October 1715*, ed. G. Holt, Catholic Record

Inevitably, once restored to the Mission, little is known about the former fellows' activities. Only the ex-president's career as vicar-apostolic in London has left visible traces. Giffard's life in the capital until the 1720s was one of considerable stress as he was continually harassed by the authorities periodically anxious to deprive the Catholic community of its spiritual leader.[55] His difficulties, however, were compounded by quarrels within the Catholic fold. In the first place, Giffard quarrelled with the London Jesuits. This was not surprising since sections of the English secular and regular clergy had long been antagonists because of the regulars' particular freedom in England from episcopal control.[56] Giffard, then, was only acting true to tradition when he did nothing to stop the appearance in 1714 of a particularly scurrilous pamphlet, *The Secret Policy of the English Society of Jesuits*, whose author was the secular priest Charles Dodd.[57] In his case, too, there were possibly personal motives. Giffard's own theological position is impossible to fathom, but it is more than likely given his training at Douai and Paris that he had little sympathy with Jesuit Molinism. Moreover in 1687 the Lime Street Chapel, run by his brother Andrew, had been handed over to the Order after the Jesuits had accused the younger Giffard of Jansenism.[58] The ex-president, therefore, had good reason to dislike the Society. As the pamphlet accused the Jesuits of conspiring to take over the English Mission, the English members of the Order were understandably annoyed at its appearance. Giffard was accused of outright connivance in the

Society, xlii (London, 1971), pp. 150-1, n; Holt, *English Jesuits*, 90; Anstruther, iii. 2-3, 35-6, 65-74, 119. Bertwisal/Hawarden also died in London in 1735; he had been on the Mission since 1707: see Anstruther, iii. 95.

55. Gillow, iii. 456; Anstruther, iii. 70-3.

56. J. Bossy, *The English Catholic Community 1570-1850* (London, 1975), pt. i.

57. *Letter Book of Lewis Sabran*, 234-6. Charles Dodd (real name Hugh Tootell, 1671-1743) was the later author of *Church History*, the first attempt to write an account of English recusant Catholicism. Dodd wrote the *Secret Policy* in the English Carthusian monastery at Nieuport: on his life, see Gillow, iv. 549-50.

58. Macray, *Register*, iv. 157. Douai was investigated for Jansenism in the first decade of the eighteenth century: see 'Dicconson's Diary' (1704-7, 1714) published in *Douai College Documents*, 71-112. Jansenism at the University of Paris was seldom embraced by the professors of theology but flourished among the simple doctors: see Brockliss, *Higher Education*, 250-4.

publication, and an ultimately ineffectual appeal was made to the nuncio in charge of the Mission in Brussels. As is clear from a letter written by one Father Eyre to Lewis Sabran, rector of St Omer's College in April 1715, Giffard by his inactivity had forfeited any respect due his position: 'Instead of a common father, he is nothing els butt a head of the opposite party.'[59]

Giffard seems to have weathered this storm fairly easily, but almost immediately he came under fresh pressure when he fell out with another member of the English hierarchy, John Talbot Stonor, bishop of Thespiae (1678-1756). In April 1716 Stonor, who had been made vicar-apostolic of the midland district the year before, obtained a papal brief replacing Giffard in his London district on the ostensible grounds of incapacity: the ex-president, now seventy-four, was judged too old and infirm to fulfil his duties.[60] The real reason, however, was political. Giffard and his friends at Douai, such as the principal George Witham, were diehard Jacobites. Faced by the accession of George I in 1714 they refused to compromise their Jacobite principles by taking an oath of loyalty to the Hanoverians. Indeed, the Old Pretender clearly relied on Giffard to keep the English Catholics true to the Stuarts:

Serenissimus Angliae rex [litteram] scribi juvit ad ilustrum et Rdssmum Episcopum Madaurensem in quo se maximam fiduciam collocare affirmabat, ut ipse conciliis et authoritate sua Catholicis in offico suo et erga ipsum obedientia retinere conarentur.[61]

Stonor and his ally Thomas Strickland (c. 1679-c. 1739), on the other hand, favoured a different approach. Although both had copied Giffard's educational example and taken a doctorate in theology at Paris, they had been only aged ten when James fled and had no vestigial loyalty to the Stuarts. Conscious that English Catholics were viewed by the state as Jacobite fifth-columnists, they therefore promoted a more realistic attitude among the faithful in the hope of gaining in return a limited

59. *Letter Book of Lewis Sabran*, 261-2. This quarrel with the Jesuits is not mentioned in any of the biographical notices devoted to Giffard.

60. *The Seventh Douai Diary 1715-1778*, ed. E. H. Burton and E. Nolan, Catholic Record Society, xxviii (London, 1928), 40-4. On Stonor, see Gillow, v. 531-2; Anstruther, iii. 211.

61. *The Seventh Douai Diary*, 75.

toleration. It was to pursue this policy that the attempt was
made to elbow Giffard aside. In their campaign Strickland and
Stonor not surprisingly found willing allies in the Jesuits, and it
was apparently the former confessor of Louis XIV, Father
Tellier, who solicited the brief from the pope.[62] There can be no
doubt that Stonor was also presenting Giffard's friends, if not
Giffard himself, as crypto-Jansenist. At the same time as the
campaign against Giffard, a declaration arrived from
Propaganda at Rome (apparently at Stonor's behest) forbidding
without papal approval the publication of the English
translation of the New Testament underway at Douai. In the
1710s translations of the Bible were definitely considered a
Jansenist fetish. In 1713 a papal bull had outlawed the reading of
the Bible in the vernacular as part of a general condemnation of
the *Nouveau Testament avec des Réflexions morales* of the
Jansenist Oratorian, Pasquier Quesnel.[63]

Stonor's attempts to displace Giffard ultimately foundered,
in part perhaps because the ex-president's Jacobite proclivities
were shared by the leading lay Catholic in England, the duke of
Norfolk.[64] As a result Giffard continued to control the London
district until his death. There can be no doubt, however, that
the struggle had left its mark on the ageing vicar-apostolic, for
in November 1720 he petitioned the pope to appoint a
coadjutor. Giffard's preference was Henry Howard, Norfolk's
brother, born in 1684, who had also been educated at Douai and
Paris and who in the late 1710s was on the Mission in London.[65]

62. Ibid. 46-7, 75. On Strickland, see Gillow, v. 533-4. Brought up at Saint-
Germain, Strickland never went on the Mission and ended his days as bishop of
Namur. Stonor and Strickland were contemporaries at Paris: Strickland was an
MA in 1707 and a licentiate of theology in 1712; Stonor was an MA in 1709:
Bibliothèque Nationale, MS Latin 9157, fos. 7 and 19; MS Latin 15440, p. 391.

63. *The Seventh Douai Diary*, 55. For the genesis of the Bull *Unigenitus*
against Quesnel, see Adam, 295-336.

64. The duke refused to take the oath in November 1719: see *The Seventh
Douai Diary*, 66. According to Anstruther, iii. 74, it was Strickland who had
pushed the government to tender the oath. Anstruther is wrong to claim that
Strickland and Stonor's pro-Hanoverian policy dated only from 1719. The
Belgian nuncio in charge of the English Mission was wanting the English clergy
to make a pro-Hanoverian declaration at least as early as December 1716: *The
Seventh Douai Diary*, 46-7.

65. Anstruther, iii. 105. The Jesuits had already tried to foist a coadjutor on
Giffard as early as 1714 in the person of Matthew Prichard OSF (1669-1750),
bishop of the western district in 1713: see *Letter Book of Lewis Sabran*, 241.

But Howard was never installed. He died suddenly, possibly even before he had received the papal brief, forcing Giffard to begin again his search for an assistant. This time his choice fell on Bernard Petre (1672-1752), an alumnus at Douai twenty years before. The pope agreed, and Giffard was presumably able to spend the final decade of his life in semi-retirement.[66]

This brief biographical history of the intruded fellows suggests an important conclusion about the character of the Magdalen fellowship in the year following the expulsion of Hough's supporters. Whatever contemporaries claimed, James II did not take advantage of the expulsion to turn Magdalen into a Catholic seminary. Even after Parker's death there was a hard core of Anglicans and Catholic fellow-travellers who cannot have been committed in the slightest to turning the college into a centre of Catholic evangelism. Presumably, then, as James had had the opportunity to create such an institution, it was never his intention to do so. Arguably, he was attempting to create a confessionally-mixed community whose members were united by a common loyalty to a divinely-appointed monarch. It was doubtless for this reason that Parker took up the office of president. It is difficult to believe that he would have accepted the position had he thought that James was going to flood the college with recusants. Admittedly, Parker is supposed to have complained on receiving the royal mandate of 24 February that he had been duped by the king who was using him as a cover to create a college of Catholics. But the story may be apocryphal.[67] Some credence, moreover, might be given to James's own insistence that he had never intended to turn the college into a papist seminary. According to the king's own apology, he had 'filled up most of the Fellowships with Catholics because few Protestants would accept them'.[68]

This point is emphasized when we look at the background of the Catholics who were introduced. Had James been seriously

66. *The Seventh Douai Diary*, p. 91; Anstruther, iii. 165-8. Petre had been chaplain to a prominent English Jacobite family. Giffard seems to have found his coadjutor somewhat of a wet blanket.

67. *Magdalen and James*, 240-1: the author of the story was a servant who was with him when he received the mandate.

68. Ibid. 270, quoted from J. S. Clarke (ed.), *The Life of James the Second Collected out of Memoirs Writ of his own Hand* (1816). The king, incorrectly, claimed that the fellowships had been filled *after* the appointment of Giffard.

interested in creating a Catholic fifth-column in the centre of Oxford he would surely have filled the vacant fellowships with well-educated clerics. To a certain extent, of course, he did this with the appointment of figures such as Fairfax and the Giffards. But the clerical graduates of Douai and Saint-Omer formed no more than half of the intake. What was the value for the cause of Catholic evangelism in elevating to fellowships laymen like Dryden, Short and the ageing Joyner? Perhaps it was intended that the youngsters amongst them, still in their early twenties, would eventually join the priesthood and form the next generation of Catholic propagandists in the university. But this seems unlikely. Had a Dryden or Short been earmarked for the priesthood they would have presumably continued their clerical training after their ejection. It is much more probable that James and his advisers had no consistent religious policy with regard to Magdalen at all. Rather, they used the unforeseen opportunity of the contumacy of Hough and his supporters to distribute largesse to Jacobite loyalists with patrons at Court. Arguably, until the intrusion of President Giffard, fellowships were simply bestowed as patronage plums to members of James's entourage. Father Petre, Sunderland and Jeffreys all probably found places for clients. As a result, a handful of highly-educated missionaries inevitably found their way into the college, but so too did a number of recent converts, Protestant loyalists and would-be men of letters.[69] Dryden's fellowship was clearly for the services rendered the Stuart and the Catholic cause by his father: only a few months before John Dryden senior had published *The Hind and the Panther*, an appropriate paeon on the benefits of a reconciliation of Canterbury and Rome.[70] A rather different reason must have lain behind the appointment of Richard Short. His father, Thomas, had been the leading Court physician in the final years

69. This point could be better substantiated if a biographical study was done of the intruded demies, for they were the fellows of the future: their names exist in the Buttery Book, but I have not yet traced their backgrounds.

70. Winn, 421-7. Dryden's poem aimed to convince the Anglicans that they should join with the Catholics in putting down the dissenters. When, shortly before its appearance, James made a bid for dissenter support by promulgating his Declaration of Indulgence (April, 1687), the polemical value of the poem was lost. Dryden, of course, had served the Stuarts well during the Exclusion crisis with his *Absalom and Achitophel*.

of Charles II's reign, and his papist tendencies led to his being threatened with expulsion from the Royal College of Physicians during the Exclusion crisis. Thomas Short had died in 1685. Presumably, the intrusion of his son was a token of royal gratitude for services rendered the royal body.[71]

But if Magdalen was not a Catholic seminary in the year 1687-8, what sort of institution was it? The answer must be, a very strange one. Perhaps unintentionally James had created a unique educational animal. In an age of religious intolerance, Magdalen had gathered within its walls a mixed community of Catholics and Protestants, clerics and laymen, regulars and seculars. Nowhere else in Europe at this date would it have been possible to find a similar educational institution. As a result, it would be pleasing to conclude that in future the history of Magdalen in the reign of James II should be seen as a chapter in the history, not of bigotry, but of ecumenicism. Such a reading of the year of the intruded fellows, however, would be anachronistic. There is no evidence that any of the fellows who inhabited the college in 1687-8 were genuine believers in toleration. Almost certainly they shared the belief of the large majority of seventeenth-century Christians, whatever the denomination, that toleration was a *pis-aller*, something to be granted only when the state was too weak to wipe out an heretical minority. In the seventeenth century everyone believed in the political and theological virtue of religious unity. Even those, like Leibniz and Bossuet, who disliked persecution, were not supporters of religious pluralism: they merely looked for ways of ending schism by finding areas of common agreement.[72] It is hard not to feel, then, that Parker's complaint against the king on receiving the February mandate would have been roundly echoed by his colleagues: 'To place me with a company of men, which he knows I hate the conversation of!'.[73] High table then must have been an uncomfortable occasion. Arguably, too, it would not just have been the Protestants and Catholics who would have ignored each other. Fairfax and the other Jesuit-educated clerics were

---

71. Munck, i. 377-9.

72. Their attempt at reconciliation is discussed in P. Hazard, *The European Mind 1680-1715*, Eng. trans. (Harmondsworth, 1975), 253-76.

73. *Magdalen and James*, 240.

doubtless at daggers drawn with the Douai contingent over the question of grace and free will, especially with the arrival of the Giffards. Was it coincidence that Fairfax gained permission to be absent for two months in the summer of 1688?[74]

In short, Magdalen in the era of the intruded fellows was almost certainly no Baconian Solomon's House, dedicated to wisdom and harmony. It must have borne a closer resemblance to Milton's Pandemonium. The ecumenical experiment could never have lasted. Whatever James's intentions, Magdalen in the climate of the late-seventeenth century would have had to become eventually a Catholic seminary run by either the regulars or seculars. Simply by transferring the power of appointment to Giffard an important step had been taken down the road to uniformity. Giffard's powers virtually guaranteed that the college would be filled henceforth with graduates from Douai.[75] The Anglicans and English Protestants generally were therefore right to be worried.

74. Magdalen College MS 730(b), Vice-President's Register, *sub* 16 July.

75. Besides appointing his own Douai-trained brother, Giffard specifically brought over to England two Douai professors, Bertwisal/Hawarden and Jones, to teach philosophy and theology. Another of his appointments was his Douai-trained chaplain, Clayton. Bertwisal/Hawarden was the only one of the intruded fellows to show any ecumenical sympathies in later life. Forced to leave Douai in 1707 on suspicion of Jansenism he devoted the rest of his life to religious controversy, publishing in particular *Charity and Truth, or Catholicks not Uncharitable in Saying that none are Saved out of the Catholick Communion, because the Rule is not Universal* (Brussels, 1728). This pamphlet claimed that all baptized Christians were members of the Catholic Church unless they had specifically apostasized.

Laurence Brockliss, Gerald Harriss, and Angus Macintyre
are Official Fellows and Tutors in Modern History
at Magdalen College, Oxford

Proceeds from the sale of this publication
will go towards the restoration of
the College's buildings

*

Produced for the President and Fellows
of Magdalen College, Oxford
by the Perpetua Press, Oxford